God's Soldiers:
Roman Catholicism and Freemasonry

by Dudley Wright

God's Soldiers:
Roman Catholicism and Freemasonry

A Cornerstone Book
Published by Cornerstone Book Publishers
An Imprint of Michael Poll Publishing
Copyright © 2006 by Cornerstone Book Publishers

Cornerstone Book Publishers
New Orleans, LA

Originally published in *The Builder Magazine* , 1921
First Cornerstone Edition - 2006
Second Cornerstone Edition 2013

www.cornerstonepublishers.com

ISBN: 1613421494
ISBN-13: 978-1-61342-149-9

MADE IN THE USA

..

Table of Contents

Foreword

Constantine the Great (c.274-337) is credited with transforming Christianity from minor cult status into a world religious power. Some say that he "fine tuned" the Bible itself and others claim that it was more of a total rewrite and religious structure edit. It is said that what was acceptable to his idea of Christianity was left in the Bible and what he considered unacceptable removed. Regardless of his influence on the texts of the Bible or the nature of Christianity itself, his actions clearly gave the Roman Catholic Church a world standing as they had never previously enjoyed. In the period following Constantine, the Church exercised its new power with sometimes ruthless fervor. This period is often described as the beginning of the Dark Ages. It was a time when to question the Church would mean torture and/or death. It was a faith ruled by an iron and often cruel fist. The Church had the final say in all aspects of life - from science, history, medicine and, of course, faith. One did not question the Church. For one to voice that the Bible was compiled by the vote of a committee of church leaders working under the supervision of a Roman Emperor some 300 years after the death of Jesus would have certainly resulted in imprisonment or death.

While time has limited the actual political authority of the Church, it remains to this day a world power. The Pope is considered and received as a head of state by most all nations with all the pomp and ceremony due a world political leader.

Freemasonry and the Roman Catholic Church have a long and never pleasant history. This work by Bro. Dudley Wright puts light upon the activities of the Church and retells the often violent persecution of Freemasonry and Freemasons by the Church. Added to the original 1921 text is the classic "Humanum Genus" by Pope Leo XIII along with Albert Pike's answer to this Papal attack upon most of society under the guise of an attack on Freemasonry.

Michael R. Poll
2006

Introduction

At frequent intervals, now for nearly two hundred years, the heads of the Roman Catholic Church have been launching their papal thunders against Freemasonry alleging that it is not only anti-Christian, but Atheistic in its constitution, that at its doors lie the many wars which have taken place during that period, and that it has been responsible for the innumerable revolutions that have disturbed nations, and the myriads of seditious plots which have been hatched, particularly since 1717, when the Mother Grand Lodge of the world was first organized. These statements, unsupported by any evidence that would be accepted in any court of law conducted on constitutional lines, have been accepted as veridical by the sheep of the flock, who have passed them along, until, finally, they have made their appearance in the bigoted press with even more embellishments than the now proverbial story of the Russians passing through England during the last war.

All these allegations can be disproved at once an examination of the Constitutions of the Craft of Freemasonry, which differs from all other societies in that it imposes a test on all applicants for admission into the Order, i. e., subscription to a belief in the existence of the Supreme Being and in the immortality of the soul. That is the test for admission into Craft, from which the member can, if he wishes his candidature is accepted, pass into the Royal Arch and Mark Masonry. But when he seeks admission in some of the so-called "side" or "higher" degrees, finds his way barred unless he declares himself to be of Christian faith, and in more than one of these has to assert, without equivocation, that he is a Trinitarian. The result is that whilst in the Craft Lodge, Arch, Mark Masonry or U.S. Scottish Rite, Jews, Christians, Mohammedans, Buddhists, Parsees, and others may be admitted, that is not possible in all branches of Masonry.

Apart from this Theistic declaration, no candidate is accepted unless he declared his allegiance to the law of the land, nor unless he declares that he will never be concerned in plots and conspiracies against the peace and welfare of the nation, and that he will behave himself conformably with the laws of his country.

Yet, in spite of these explicit obligations, which have to be taken by all, without exception, we find Popes and Prelates who, during the last two centuries, have been repeating times innumerable that Freemasonry in every country is engaged, if not solely, at least principally, in a warfare against Church and State. The papal denunciations have been repeated parrot-like by the lesser lights and believed in by the multitude, who are inhibited from seeking authentic information at the fountain head.

Thus, for instance, Monsignor Dillon, D. D., in his "War of Antichrist with the Church," says:

"Every secret society is framed and adapted to make men the enemies of God and His Church, and to subvert faith; and there is not one, no matter on what pretext it may be founded, which does not fall under the management of a Supreme Directorate governing all secret societies on earth. The one aim of this Directorate is to uproot Christianity and the Christian social order, as well as the Church from the world - in fact, to eradicate the name of Christ and the very Christian idea from the minds and the hearts of men."

Monsignor Dillon obliges by giving the names of one or two of the "Grand Directors" to whom he refers as governing the whole of the secret societies of the world, the Craft of Freemasonry included. Only one name need concern us in this investigation; it is that of the late Brother John Yarker, a very distinguished scholar, who held many important offices in what are known as the "higher degrees," but who never attained rank in the United Grand Lodge of England. He was also a member of and held high office in certain quasi-Masonic bodies not recognized by the Grand Lodge of England. Now has any one of the clergy of the Roman Catholic Church, who repeats this absurd statement about a Grand Directorate as set forth by Monsignor Dillon, considered the position for a moment? John Yarker is said to have been Grand Director during part of the time of the Grand Mastership of the late King Edward VII, and the present ruler, H. R. H., the Duke of Connaught. Can any man in his right mind imagine either of these exalted personages receiving and obeying instructions from John Yarker, or, indeed, any other individual? The assertion is so ridiculous as to carry with it its own refutation.

The statement is also made repeatedly by Roman Catholic controversialists that Freemasonry is international and that members of English lodges are at liberty to enter, and fraternize with the members of, any and every lodge throughout the world. Freemasonry is international up to a point. There are certain landmarks set forth in the Ancient Charges which must not be departed from, if Freemasonry in its original institution, so far as can be ascertained, is to be upheld, and no English Freemason is to be permitted, under pain of expulsion, to enter any lodge where those ancient landmarks are not observed. Freemasonry may be described as a religious institution, but not as a religion. Its most ancient landmark is the recognition of, and belief in, the existence of a Supreme Being. It was the deletion of this fundamental tenet on the part of the Grand Orient of France and other Jurisdictions, which led to the United Grand Lodge of England and other Masonic Grand Bodies, to cease communication with them, and to prohibit inter-visitation, which ban holds good at the present moment.

Since the constitution of the Grand Lodge of England in 1717, many eminent members of the Roman Catholic Church have held office in the Grand Lodge of England. Some have even been appointed to the highest possible position - that of Grand Master. Among others, we have the name of Robert Edward, Lord Petre, who was regarded as the head of the Roman Catholic body in this country in his time, and who was Grand Master from 1772 to 1776, presiding over a Society against which the thunders of the Vatican had been launched at least twice before that time, thus proving that in England, at any rate, the Papal fulminations had been of no effect.

A writer in the *Weekly Register* (a Roman Catholic organ) in 1865, said:

"Cardinal Wiseman, with his natural kindness of heart, never spoke unkindly of English Freemasonry, and two of his predecessors (then known as Vicars-Apostolic) were active members of London lodges. Two members of the present English Hierarchy are understood to have been initiated in their early days and I can vouch for two influential members of English Chapters (meaning Canons) being also Freemasons." It is an open secret, also, that the Papal Bulls are equally ineffective in their prohibition in many instances at the present day.

Sir Charles Cameron, Deputy Grand Master of Ireland, in his annual statement to the Grand Lodge of Ireland, in 1919, made the following announcement:

"It is an extraordinary thing how common is the opinion that Freemasonry is opposed to the Roman Catholic religion. We know that a great many members of that community formerly belonged to our Order. I had the pleasure of meeting three Roman Catholic judges - Judge Keogh, Lord Morris, and Lord Justice Barry - at Masonic dinners on several occasions, about some forty or fifty years ago - before some of you were born. We know that the Roman Catholics have seceded from us because they were obliged to do so by the direction of their Church, but many of them have told me they would like to become Freemasons if they were permitted to join the Order. There are thousands of Freemasons in purely Roman Catholic countries. Ninety per cent of the French population are members of the Roman Catholic Church - nominally, at all events - and still Masonry flourishes in France, and also in other Roman Catholic countries. In Ireland, at all events, we are a nonpolitical body in every sense of the word, and equally nonsectarian."

It is somewhat tedious, however, to wade through the mass of misrepresentations which present themselves on every occasion when the Roman clergy venture upon expositions of Freemasonry. Monsignor de Segur in his work, *La Franc-Maconnerie*, says that in order to be admitted to certain Masonic lodges, it is indispensable that the candidate should bring with him a particle of the Adorable Sacrament, which he must procure by some means or the other, and that the fist act of initiation consists in trampling on it. He assures his readers that this horrible rite is performed in several lodges of Paris, Marseilles, Aix,

Avignon, Lyons, Chalons, and Laval, cities and towns where the greatest piety exists and which are, above all others, the nuclei of Roman Catholic life and devotion in France. He describes a Masonic Mass, celebrated in Rome, on an altar lighted by six candles of black wax. Each member was obliged to take with him a consecrated Host, and all these Hosts were placed in a receptacle on a table, while every new candidate trod on a crucifix, spat on it, and, finally, drawing his dagger, struck repeated blows on the sacred pieces.

Many will shudder involuntarily when these lines are read, and would that it were not necessary to write them, for no Freemason would, or could, if bound by his undertaking, ever be a party to the reviling of any faith or creed or to such a dastardly outrage as Monsignor de Segur describes. Let him be assured that whatever may have been the organization to which such horrible fiends belonged, it certainly was not Masonry.

In subsequent installments of this article the various Bulls, Allocutions, and Encyclical Letters of the Popes on Freemasonry and other Societies will be given, with details of the oral examinations of, and the tortures inflicted by, "the Holy Office of the Inquisition," together with particulars of other persecutions of Freemasons by the "Holy Catholic and Apostolic Church."

The question as to the cause of the hostility of the Church of Rome towards the Masonic Order has often been the theme of discussion and debate, with the attainment of no definite result. It may not be possible to fix with accuracy the date of the origin of the Masonic Craft, but few today would dispute its continuance through the Middle Ages in the Craft or Trade Guilds of England and other countries. Religion figured largely in the proceedings of these Guilds, many of their ceremonies taking place in the Guild Chapels. The Guildsmen were devout Roman Catholics, which accounts for the fact that the waning power of the Guilds is distinctly traceable in its origin to the period of the Reformation. The occasional references and allusions to the "Masonic Society" in various writings also date their commencement to the same period. These references became increasingly numerous until 1717, when Freemasonry became an organized constitution, to be honored, shortly after its establishment in this manner, with the promulgation of a Bull by Clement XII. The Guilds performed "misteries"; their membership was limited; oaths had to be taken on admission and on certain occasions afterwards; their proceedings were conducted in secrecy, but the Roman Church issued no Bull against these societies. But when Freemasons did these things, they were wrong; nay, more, they became a menace to Society and to the Church. The Church of Rome raises no objection to secret societies when they are composed of its members - they have always existed in the Catholic Church, they exist today - but when conformity to the Roman Church and its doctrines is not made a test for admission, then the society is inimical to the morals and well-being of the nation.

Lawrie (the pseudonym of Sir David Brewster in his *History of Freemasonry*, states that "in order to encourage the profession of architecture, the bishop of Rome and the other potentates of Europe conferred on the Fraternity of Freemasons the most important privileges; and allowed them to be governed by law customs, and ceremonies peculiar to themselves." This condition of things, however, did not last, and he goes on to point out that "in after ages, when Masons were more numerous, and when the demand for religious structures was less urgent than before, the bishops of Rome deprived the Fraternity of those very privileges which had been conferred on them without solicitation and persecuted with unrelenting rage the very men whom they had voluntarily taken into favor, and who had contributed to the grandeur of their ecclesiastic establishment." Possibly, however, the reason for the inhibition is due less to the cause assigned by Lawrie that "secret associations, indeed, are always a terror temporal and spiritual tyranny" than to the personnel of the new organization. For it must not be forgotten that two of the most active workers in the early day of the history of the Grand Lodge of England - before the issue of the first Papal Bull against Freemasons or the inauguration of any concerted opposition to the Craft - were Dr. J.T. Desaguliers and the Rev. Dr. James Anderson, the former the son of a French refugee Hugenot minister and the latter a Scotch Presbyterian minister, neither of whom, in private life, could have any sympathy with, but rather opposition to, Roman Catholic claims and pretensions.

The earliest Masonic inhibitions were not, however, the work - directly, at any rate - of the Church of Rome. Most writers give the date of the initial prohibition as 1735, with Holland as the venue. Llorente in his *History of the Inquisition*, assigns an earlier date. Llorente may be regarded as a reliable authority, since he was secretary of the Inquisition at Madrid from 1789 to 1791 and, therefore, had access to original documents and records. He says:

"The first severe measure against Freemasons in Europe was that decreed on 14th December, 1732, by the Chamber of Police of the Chatelet at Paris: it prohibited Freemasons from assembling, and condemned M. Chapelot to a penalty of 6,000 livres for having suffered them to assemble in his house. Louis XV commanded that those peers of France, and other gentlemen who had the privilege of the entry, should be deprived of that honor, if they were members of a Masonic lodge. The Grand Master of the Parisian lodges being obliged to quit France, convoked an assembly of Freemasons to appoint his successor. Louis XV, on being informed of this, declared that if a Frenchman was elected, he would send him to the Bastille. However, the Due D'Antin was chosen and, after his death, Louis de Bourbon, prince of Conti, succeeded him. Louis de Bourbon, due de Chartres, another prince of the blood, became Grand Master."

Masonic persecutions took their rise in Holland in the year 1735. The States-General became alarmed at the rapid increase of Freemasons, who held their meetings in every town under their government; and as they could not believe that architecture and brotherly love were their only objects, they resolved to discountenance their proceedings. In consequence of this determination, an edict was issued by government stating that though they had discovered nothing in the practices of the Fraternity, either injurious to the interests of the Republic, or contrary to the character of good citizens; yet, in order to prevent any bad consequences which might ensue from such association, they deemed it prudent to abolish the assemblies of Freemasons. Notwithstanding this prohibition a respectable lodge having continued to meet privately at Amsterdam, intelligence was communicated to the magistrates, who arrested all the members; and brought them to the Court of Justice. Before this tribunal, in presence of all the magistrates of the city, the Master and Wardens boldly defended themselves; and declared upon oath that they were loyal subjects, faithful to their religion, and zealous for the interests of their country; that Freemasonry was an institution venerable in itself and useful to society; and that though they could not reveal the secrets and ceremonies of their Order, they would assure them that they were contrary to the laws neither of God nor man, and that they would willingly admit into their Order any individual in whom the magistrates could confide, and from whom they might receive such information as would satisfy a reasonable mind. In consequence of these declarations, the brethren were dismissed, and the town secretary requested to become a member of the Fraternity. After initiation, he returned to the Court of Justice and gave such a favorable account of the principles and practices of the Society that all the magistrates became brethren of the Order and zealous patrons of Freemasonry.

In the same year - 1735 - several noble Portuguese, with more foreigners, instituted a lodge in Lisbon under the Grand Lodge of England, of which George Gordon was Master, but no sooner was the slightest suspicion entertained of its existence, than the clergy determined to give the clearest evidence of their hatred to the Order by practical illustration.

The Elector Palatine of the Rhine also prohibited the Order in his States and arrested several members at Mannheim, in consequence of their disobedience.

Masonic assemblies were also abolished in France in 1737 under the pretext that beneath their inviolable secrets they might cover some dreadful designs hostile to religion and dangerous to the kingdom.

The Grand Lodge of England, regarded by all Freemasons as the Mother Grand Lodge of the world, was not founded until 1717, but Joseph Lavallee in his Histoire des Inquisitions Religeuqes d'Italie, d'espagne, et de Portugal, says that, in 1710, Nicholas Augustan de Seras, merchant, of Cette was charged before the Inquisition at Vallodolid with being a "sorcerer Freemason," and that in 1722 one John Lilburn was brought to the auto-da-fe at Lisbon on the same charge, it being stated that he had assisted at nocturnal meetings where the demon Gamaliel presided in person and that he (Lilbum) had drank and eaten in company of other demons brought from the infernal regions, with whom he had afterwards signed a pact, promising to be their servant and to perform all that they should order him to do.

Freemasonry, also, was not under the ban of the Church when its introduction into Tuscany led the Grand Duke Gian Gastone to prohibit it. His death on 9th July, 1737, caused his edict to be neglected. This demise, however, had another result as well. The clergy represented the matter to Pope Clement XII, who sent an inquisitor to Florence, who made a number of arrests, but the offenders were set at liberty by the new Grand Duke, Francis of Lorraine, who declared himself the patron of the Order and participated in the organization of several lodges. At this time the Papal Court began to make a stir about Freemasons. We find the Pope in consultation with Cardinals Ottobone, Spinola, and Zondedari, and the Inquisitor of Florence, and on 28th April, 1738, Clement XII issued his famous Bull on the subject. In this document the only accusation brought against the Craft is its secrecy, but this was sufficient for the creation of a new heresy, furnishing the Inquisition with a fresh subject for its activity.

The Bull was as follows:

"The Condemnation of the Societies or Conventicles De Liberi Muretori, or of the Freemasons, under the penalty of *ipso facto* Excommunication, the Absolution from which is reserved to the Pope alone, except at the point of death.

"Clement, Bishop, servant of the Apostles of God, to all the faithful of Christ, health and apostolical benediction.

"Placed (unworthy as we are) by the disposal of the divine clemency, in the eminent watchtower of the apostolic see, we are ever solicitously intent, agreeable to the trust of the pastoral providence reposed in us, by obstructing the passages of error and vice, to preserve more especially the integrity of the orthodox religion, and to repel, in these difficult times, all danger of trouble from the whole Catholic world.

"It has come to our knowledge, even from public report, that certain societies, companies, meetings, assemblies, clubs, or conventicles, called De Liberi Muretori, or 'Freemasons,' or by whatsoever name the same in different languages are distinguished, spread far and wide, and are every day increasing; in which persons, of whatever religion or sect, contented with a kind of affected show of natural honesty, confederate together in a close and inscrutable bond, according to laws and orders agreed upon between them; which, likewise, with private ceremonies, they enjoin and bind themselves, as well by strict oath taken on the Bible, as by the imprecations of heavy punishments to preserve with inviolable secrecy.

"We, therefore, resolving in our minds the great mischiefs which generally accrue from these kind of societies or conventicles, not only to the temporal tranquillity of the State, but to the spiritual health of souls; and that, therefore, they are neither consistent with civil nor canonical sanctions; since we are taught by the divine word to watch, like a faithful servant, night and day, lest this sort of men break as thieves into the house, and like foxes endeavour to root up the vineyard; lest they should pervert the hearts of the simple, and privately shoot at the innocent, that we might stop up the broad way, which from thence would be laid open for the perpetration of their wickedness with impunity, and for other just and reasonable causes to be known, have, by advice of some of our venerable brethren of the Roman Church, the Cardinals, and of our own mere notion, and from our certain knowledge and mature deliberation, by the plenitude of the apostolical power, appointed and decreed to be condemned and prohibited and this by our ever-present valid constitution, we do condemn and prohibit the same societies, companies, meetings, assemblies, clubs, or conventicles, De Liberi Muretori, or Freemasons, or by what other name they are distinguished or known.

"Wherefore all and singular, the faithful in Christ, of whatever state, degree, condition, order, dignity, and it preeminence, whether laity or clergy, as well seculars as regulars, worthy all of express mention and enumeration, we strictly and in virtue or holy obedience, command that no one, under any pretext or color, dare or presume the aforesaid societies, De Liberi Muretori, or Freemasons, or by whatever other manner distinguished, to enter into, promote, flavor, admit, or conceal in his or their houses, or elsewhere, or be admitted members of, or be present, with the same, or be anywise aiding and assisting towards their meeting in any place; or to administer anything to them, or in any means publicly or privately, directly or indirectly, by themselves or others, afford them counsel, help, or favor; or advise, induce, provoke, or persuade others to be admitted into, joined or be present with these kind of societies, or in any manner aid and promote them; but that they ought by all means to abstain from the said societies, under the penalty of all that act contrary thereto, incurring excommunication ipso facto, without any other declaration: from which no one can obtain the benefit of absolution from any other but us, or the Roman Pontiff for the time being, except at the point of death.

"We will, moreover, and command, that as well bishops and superior prelates, and other ordinaries of particular places, as the inquisitors of heretical pravity universally adopted, of what state, degree, condition, order, dignity, or preeminence soever, proceed and inquire, and restrain and coerce the same, as vehemently suspected of heresy with condign punishment for to them, and each of them, we hereby give and impart free power of proceeding, inquiring against, and of coercing and restraining with condign punishment, the same transgressors, and of calling in, if it shall be necessary, the help of the secular arm; and we will that printed copies of these presents, signed by some notary public, and confirmed by the seal of some person of ecclesiastical dignity, shall be of the same authority as original letters would be, if they were shown and exhibited. Let no one, therefore, infringe, or by rash attempt contradict this object of our declaration, damnation, command, prohibition, and interdict; but if anyone shall presume to attempt this, let him know that he will incur the anger of Almighty God, and of the blessed apostles Peter and Paul.

"Dated from Rome at St. Mary's the Greater, in the year of the Incarnation of our Lord, 1738, the fourth of the calends of May (28th April, N.S.) in the eighth of our pontificate."

The Bull was fixed up and published at the gates of the palace of the Sacred Office of the prince of the Apostles and in the usual and accustomed places of the city by Peter Romolatius, arm of the Most Holy Inquisition.

Less than a week afterwards - on the 4th May, 1838 - the Bishops of Siga, Cambysopolis, Trachis, and Olena - titular bishops in England - published an episcopal denunciation of Freemasonry, stating:

"We enjoin that the Catholics be discreetly warned against entering into the Society of them who are vulgarly called 'Freemasons,'" and, in April, 1842, the bishop of Olena promulgated an injunction to be observed in the London district declaring that by a response of the Sacred Congregation of the Holy Office, 5th July, 1837, it hath been declared that "a confessor cannot lawfully or validly, grant sacramental absolution to men belonging to the Society of Freemasons, who are incorporated under, and mutually bound by, the obligation of an oath of secrecy, unless they absolutely, positively, and forever, abandon the aforesaid condemned society. This rule must be implicitly followed, where the penitent is avowedly associated with the body of Freemasons, or where, in confession, he declares himself to be a Freemason."

In the year following the promulgation of the Bull - on 14th January, 1739 - the Cardinal Secretary of State issued an edict pronouncing irremissible pain of death, not only on all members, but on all who should tempt others to join the Order or should rent a house to it or flavor it in any other way. This decree was issued in the name of the High Priest of the God of Peace and Mercy! It was as follows:

"EDICT - Joseph Cardinal Firrao, of the title of St. Thomas in Parione, and of the Sacred Roman College, Cardinal Priest.

"Whereas the holiness of our sovereign lord Pope, Clement XII, happily reigning, in his Bull of the 28th April last, beginning In eminenti, condemned, under pain of excommunication reserved to himself, certain companies, societies, and meetings, under the title of Freemasons, more properly to be called conventicles, which, under the pretext of civil society, tempt men of any sect and religion, with the strict tie of secrecy, confirmed by oath on the sacred Bible, as to all that is transacted or done in the said meetings and conventicles; and whereas such societies, meetings, and conventicles are not only suspect of occult heresy, but even dangerous to the public peace, and the safety of the ecclesiastic state, since if they do not contain matters contrary to the orthodox faith, to the state, and to the peace of the commonwealth, so many and strict ties of secrecy would not be required, as it is wisely taken notice of in the aforesaid Bull; and it being the will of the holiness of our said lord, that such societies, meetings, and conventicles totally cease and be dissolved, and that they who are not constrained by the fear of censures, be curbed at least by temporal punishment.

"Therefore, it is the express order of his holiness, by this edict to prohibit all persons of any class, state, or condition soever, whether ecclesiastical, secular, or regular, of whatever institute, degree, or dignity, though ordinarily or extraordinarily privileged, even such as require special mention to be made of them, comprehending the four legations of Bologna, Ferrara, Romagna Urbino, and the city and dukedom of Benevento; and it is hereby forbidden that any do presume to meet, assemble, or associate in any place under the said societies, or assemblies of Freemasons or under any title or cloak whatsoever, or even be present at such meetings and assemblies, under pain of death and confiscation of their effects, to be irremissibly incurred without hopes of grace.

"It is likewise prohibited, as above, to any person soever to seek or tempt anyone to associate with any such societies, meetings, or assemblies, or to advise, aid, or abet to the like purpose, the said meetings or assemblies, under the penalties above said; and they who shall furnish or provide a house, or any other place, for such meetings or conventicles to be held, though under pretext of loan, hire or any other contract soever, are hereby condemned, over and above the aforesaid penalties, to have the house or houses, or other places where such meetings and conventicles shall be held, utterly erased and demolished; and it is the will of his holiness that to incur the above said penalty of demolition, any human conjectures, hints, or presumptions, may and shall suffice for the presumption of knowledge in the landlords of such houses and places, without admission of any excuse soever.

"And because it is the express will of our said lord that such meetings, societies, and conventicles do cease, as pernicious and suspect of heresy and sedition, be utterly dissolved; his holiness does hereby strictly order that any persons as above, who shall have notice for the future of the holding of such meetings, assemblies, and conventicles, or who shall be solicited to associate with the same, or are in any manner accomplices or partakers with them, be obliged under the fine of a thousand crowns in gold, besides other grievous corporal punishments, the allies not to be excepted, to be inflicted at pleasure, to denounce them to his eminence, or to the chief magistrate of the ordinary tribunal of the cities, or other places in which the offence shall be committed, contrary to this edict; with promise and assurance to such denouncers or informers, that they shall be kept inviolably secret and safe, and shall farther obtain grace and immunity, notwithstanding any penalty they themselves may or shall have incurred.

"And that none may excuse himself from the obligation of conforming under the borrowed pretext of only secret, of the most sacred oath, or other stricter tie, by the order of his said holiness, notice is hereby given, to all, that such obligation of any secret, or any sort of oath in criminal matters, and already condemned under pain of excommunication, as above, neither holds nor binds in any manner, being null and void and of no force.

"It is our will that the present edict, when affixed in the usual places in Rome, do oblige and bind Rome and its district, and from the term of twenty-one days after, the whole ecclesiastical state, comprehending even the cities of Bologna, Ferrara, and Benevento, in the same manner as if they had been personally notified to each of them.

"Given in Rome this 14th January, 1739."

In July, 1738, the Chief of the Inquisition in Lisbon, having learned of the existence of Freemasons in that city, applied to several persons whom he believed to have knowledge of their proceedings, with the object of ascertaining definite information on the point. The first to whom he appealed was Charles O'Kelly, professor of theology, at the College of Corpo Santo, who stated that in a restaurant in the Rue de Remolares, belonging to an Irishman named Rice, there was held a Masonic lodge, attended by several individuals, many of whose names he gave, declaring at the same time that they were excellent Roman Catholics, judging by their constant attendance at the services held in the Church of Corpo Santo. The persons indicated were questioned, when they at once admitted their membership of and frequent attendance at the lodge in question, declaring that there was nothing in the Masonic ceremonies contrary to their religion, but that as they were good Roman Catholics they would obey the Holy Father and abandon Freemasonry, since the Pope had condemned it. The following were, at the same time, denounced by them to the Inquisition: Hugh O'Kelly, a retired Irish Colonel and Master of the lodge at that time; Lieutenant Denis Hogan of the Alcantara cavalry; Thomas French, merchant; James O'Kelly, dancing master to the royal family; Michael O'Kelly, his brother, owner of glass works; Charles Carroll, merchant; Sergeant-major Charles Mardel, a German engineer; and three Dominicans, Fathers Patrick O'Kellan (or Kinide), Tilan, and Leynan. They were all questioned and their replies, which are on record, are of interest to the Masonic historian. The Master, Hugh O'Kelly, who was interrogated three times, declared that Freemasonry had existed in Portugal since 1733, having been introduced into that country by a Scotsman named Gordon; that he had been initiated two years previously, but had only attended a lodge entirely composed of Roman Catholics, which was known as "La Maison Royale des Francs-Macons de la Lusitanie," which had no connection with the Protestant lodges, of which he knew nothing; that their meetings were held on the first Wednesday of each month; and that their discussions were limited to subjects of general interest, economical and recreative questions; that the lodge practised three degrees, Apprentice, Companion, and Master, but that meetings in two other grades - Excellent Master and Grand Master - were held once in every year; that they observed the festival of St. John, but that, in obedience to the pontifical interdict, the lodge had been dissolved and that the majority of the members had abandoned Freemasonry. A minority had, he believed, affiliated with a Protestant lodge, but their names were unknown to him. Thereupon, the Inquisition abandoned its pursuit of Roman Catholic Freemasons but sought to obtain further information with respect to the Protestant lodges.

Dudley Wright
1921

God's Soldiers:
Roman Catholicism and Freemasonry

Chapter I

THE FIRST victim of the Pope's savage decree is said to have been a Frenchmen, the author of a book entitled *An Apology for the Society of Freemasons*. The book was ordered to be burnt by the Ministers of Justice in one of the most frequented streets of Rome. The papal decree concerning this offender was worded as follows:

"18th February, 1739. The Sacred Congregation of the most eminent and most reverend Cardinals of the Holy Roman See and Inquisitor-General in the Christian republic against heretical provity, held in the convent of St. Mary Minervam, thoroughly weighing that a certain book, written in French, small in its size, but most wicked in regard to its bad subject, entitled *The History of and an Apology for the Society of Freemasons*, By J. G. D. M. F. M., printed at Dublin for Patrick Odoroke, 1739, has been published to the great scandal of all the faithful in Christ, in which book there is an apology for the society of Freemasons, already justly condemned by the Holy See; after a mature examination thereof, a censure, and that to be by our most holy lord, Pope Clement XII, together with the suffrages of the most eminent and most reverend lords, the Cardinals, by the command of his holiness, condemns and prohibits, by the present decree, the said book, as containing propositions and wicked principles.

"Wherefore that so hurtful and wicked a work may be abolished, as much as possibly it can, or at least that it may not continue without the perpetual note of infamy, the same Sacred Congregation, by command as above has ordered that the said work shall be burnt publicly by the Minister of Justice in the street of St. Mary supra Minervam, on the 25th of the current month, at the same time the congregation shall be held in the convent of the same St. Mary.

"Moreover, this same Sacred Congregation, by the command of his holiness, positively forbids and prohibits all the faithful in Christ, that none dare by any means, and under any pretence whatsoever, copy, print, or cause to be copied or printed or written, or presume to read the said book in any language and version now published or (which God forbid) may be published hereafter, and now condemned by this decree, under the pain of excommunication, to be incurred *ipso facto* by those who shall offend therein; but that they shall presently and effectually deliver it up to the ordinaries of such places, or to the inquisitors of heretical pravity, who shall burn it, or cause it to be burnt, without delay.

"Paul Antinus Capellorius, notary-public of the Holy Roman and Universal Inquisition."

Archibald Bower, who was Counsellor of the Inquisition at Macerata, in his *History of the Popes* published in 1768, says that Clement XII (who was a Florentian named Lawrence Corsini) "began his Pontificate with obliging

1

Cardinal Corsica, and those whom he had employed, to give an account of their late administration, and answer the many accusations brought against them by persons of all ranks and condition. They were tried by a particular Congregation appointed for that purpose, and it plainly appearing that they had defrauded the Apostolic Chamber of immense sums, they were sentenced to make them good which reduced them almost to beggary. We are told that a very small share of the sums which they were forced to refund came into the Apostolic Chamber, His Holiness having privately disposed of it to his nephews and relatives.... He was a man of learning and an encourager, of the learned, but left no writings behind him besides some Bulls, and among these one, allowing the Protestants who should embrace the Roman Catholic religion to continue in the possession of the Church lands which they held before their conversion. He improved the Vatican Library with a noble collection of scarce and valuable books."

Bower, it may be stated, resigned his office in the Inquisition and left the Church of Rome because of the treatment meted out to an innocent Man who was driven mad by his sufferings in the prison of the Inquisition and of a nobleman who expired under the hands of his torturers, of both of which inhuman and shocking scenes he was an eyewitness.

In the same year also the Inquisition tortured a Mason, one Dr. Crudeli, Master of the Florence Lodge, and kept him in prison for a considerable time. He suffered the most unmerited cruelties for maintaining the innocence of the Association. When the Grand Lodge of England was informed of his miserable situation, they decided that a foreigner, whatever his rank, had claim upon their sympathy, and they transmitted to him the sum of twenty pounds for procuring the necessaries of life and they also exerted every nerve for effecting his liberation. The death penalty was, however, a matter for the secular authorities and not under the control of the Inquisition, so far as Florence was concerned. It was not until December of that year that the Grand Lodge of England succeeded in their negotiations for the freedom of Dr. Crudeli, through the new Grand Duke, Francis Stephen, subsequently Francis I of Austria, who had been initiated into the Order in 1731 at the Hague. When afterwards the Inquisition offered pardon for self-denunciation and a hundred crowns for information, and made several arrests, the Grand Duke interposed and liberated the prisoners.

The papal commands were eagerly welcomed in Spain and the Bull received the royal approval there, while the Inquisitor-general, Orbe y Larreategui, published it in an edict dated 11th October, 1738, pointing out that the Inquisition had exclusive jurisdiction in this matter. He called for denunciation within six days of all infractions under pain of excommunication and of a fine of two hundred ducats. The edict was ordered to be read in the churches and to be affixed to their portals. Then arose a conflict between the spiritual and secular powers. In 1740, Philip V issued an edict under which a number of Masons were sent to the galleys, while the Inquisition vindicated its rights by breaking up a lodge in Madrid and insisting upon punishing its members. Freemasons were thus the victims whichever party issued the decree.

It is sometimes asserted by Catholic writers that the Inquisition was a purely secular organization, so that it may be of interest to record its actual constitution.

The reigning Pope was the head of the Inquisition, which was known in Rome as the Holy Office: he nominated all the Cardinals who composed this Congregation. He also nominated all the presiding Inquisitors of the secondary tribunals. They held their office at the will of the Pope, who had the power of deposing them from their office without acquainting them of the cause of their disgrace. The Holy Office at Rome was composed of Cardinals and Consultors. The Cardinals formed the tribunal: they were the judges, the Consultors composed the jury and had to be Canonists or regular priests. Each subordinate tribunal was composed of three judges, three secretaries, a sergeant-major, and three consulters, except in Italy, where the tribunal was composed of an Inquisitor, assisted by a Vicar, a Fiscal, a Notary and some Consulters. Each of these tribunals had several gaolers and a large number of other officers. An Inquisitor had to prove his descent from an old-established Catholic family, none of whose ancestors had been charged before a tribunal. An oath of fidelity to preserve the secrets of the Inquisition had to be taken, and the violation of this meant the death penalty, no excuse being possible nor was there any appeal in mitigation of the sentence allowed.

The Inquisition was empowered by the Pope to deal with (1), heretics; (2), those suspected of heresy; (3), their abettors, protectors, and all persons who had shown them any favor; (4), magicians, sorcerers, enchanters, and those who made use of witchcraft; (5), blasphemers; (6), persons accused of having resisted the officers of the Inquisition, or of having questioned the jurisdiction of that body. Under the name of heretics were included all who had written, taught, or preached anything contrary to the Holy Scriptures, symbols and articles of faith, the traditions of the Church, those who had left the Roman Catholic Church and embraced another faith, those Roman Catholics who had praised the practices or ceremonies of other cults, those who were of opinion that good was to be found in all religions, if faithfully practised and good faith exercised, those who uttered or taught any opinion contrary to the sovereign and illimitable authority of the Pope, or who denied that the power of the Pope was above that of the temporal power of princes and monarchs: in short, any who questioned or criticized the ultimatum of the Pope on any subject whatever.

In 1740, the Roman Catholic priests in Holland attempted to enforce obedience to the commands of their superiors. Penitents who came to confession were asked if they were Freemasons: if they were, the certificate for Holy Communion was refused and they were expelled forever from the Communion table. After a time, however, the States-General interfered and prohibited the clergy from asking questions that were unconnected with the religious character of the individual penitent.

Acting under papal compulsion, the Grand Master of Malta in 1740 caused the *Bull of Clement XII* to be published in that island and forbade the meetings of the Freemasons. In 1741, the Inquisition pursued the Freemasons at Malta. The Grand Master proscribed their assemblies under severe penalties and six Knights of Malta were banished from the island in perpetuity for having assembled at a meeting.

A lodge had been opened in Rome on 15th August, 1735. It worked in English, but in 1737, under the Mastership of the Earl of Wintoun, the Inquisition seized its serving brethren and it was closed on 20th August of that year. In the archives of the Grand Lodge of Scotland is an old parchment-bound Minute-book with the following explanatory memorandum prefixed by a brother named Andrew Lumsden, dated Edinburgh, 20th November, 1799:

"Pope Clement the twelfth having published a most severe edict against Masonry, the last lodge held at Rome was on the 20th August, 1738, when the late Earl of Wintoun was Master. The officer of the lodge, who was a servant of Dr. James Irvin, was sent, as a terror to others, prisoner to the Inquisition, but was soon released. This happened about twelve years before I went to Rome, otherwise I should no doubt have been received as I was a brother of the Lodge of Edinburgh Dunfermline.

"This record of the Roman lodge remained, after its suppression, in the hands of the Earl of Wintoun, till his death in December, 1750, when it was given by his Lordship's executors to Dr. Irvin, the only brother of that lodge then remaining at Rome; and who, I believe, wrote its original statutes in Latin.

"After the death of Dr. Irvin, his widow gave the record to me, as she had heard her husband call me 'brother.' I carefully preserved it, till I delivered it at Paris to John Macgowan, Esq., to be by him given to my cousin, Sir Alexander Dick, of Prestonfield, Baronet, who, before the death of his brother, Sir William Dick, was known by the name of Dr. Alexander Cunningham, and belonged to the Roman lodge.

"After the death of Sir Alexander Dick, his son, the late Sir William, returned it to Mr. Macgowan, who now put it into the hands of the Right Honorable Sir James Stirling, Baronet, Lord Provost of Edinburgh, and Grand Master of Scotland, to be, by his lordship, deposited among the archives of the Grand Lodge.

"Such is the progress of this record, which is attested by Andrew Lumsden."

After Clement XII had issued his Bull in 1738 many Freemasons in the Romanist States of Germany founded, at Vienna the Order of the Mopses, admitting both men and women to membership, and claiming to be devoted to the papacy. According to some writers the founder of this Order was the Duke of Bavaria, himself a Freemason. The title is undoubtedly derived from the German mops, meaning "a young mastiff," which representation is also claimed to have been the badge of the Order, symbolic of fidelity and attachment.

In 1743, King John V of Portugal was persuaded by his entourage that the Freemasons were heretics and rebels and he issued an edict against them. An era of persecution and torture at the hands of the Inquisition followed, the best known case and the one of which the fullest particulars are available being that of John Coustos. After his release from prison Coustos published a full narrative of his arrest and subsequent tortures, and the following story is given in his own words:

"Being desirous of furnishing my readers with every possible proof that I actually underwent the tortures narrated in these pages, I submit the wounds, still visible upon my arms and legs, to the inspection of Dr. Hoadley and to Mr. Hawkins, and Mr. Carey, surgeons; and I feel grateful to those gentlemen for having authorized me to state that they are quite satisfied the marks resulted from great and peculiar violence, and that their position corresponds exactly with the tortures hereinafter described.

"I am a native of Berne, in Switzerland, and a lapidary by profession. In the year 1716, my father came with his family to London, and easily obtained there letters of naturalization.

"After twenty-two years' residence I went to Paris, and worked for the French king in the galleries of the Louvre. Having thus spent five years, I removed to Lisbon, with the ultimate design of settling in the Brazils, allured by the vision of gold and jewels so abundant there, and the certainty of acquiring a fortune. But the King of Portugal, by advice of his council, deemed it impolitic to permit a foreign lapidary roam through a colony abounding with precious stones of whose value and extent the government labor to keep even their own subjects in ignorance. At Lisbon therefore, I was content to settle, having lost all hopes of being permitted to emigrate. Employment in my profession I found in abundance, and soon could have amassed a competency, for age, had I escaped the cruel grasp of the bloodthirsty inquisitors. These tyrants detain at the post office the letters of all about whom they entertain suspicions. Mine, they intercepted, hoping to discover some allusion to Freemasonry, I being notorious as one of the most zealous professors of that art. Not discovering, however, any passages which struck at the Romish religion, or tended to disturb the government, yet still bent upon the discovery of the Masonic secret, they resolved to seize one of the leading brethren, and I was selected being the Master of a lodge. With

5

me they associated the Warden, Mr. Alexander James Monton, a diamond cutter, born in Paris, and a Romanist. He had been settled six years in Lisbon, where he was jeweler to the court.

"The reader must know that our lodges in Lisbon were not held at taverns, etc., but alternately at the private dwellings of chosen friends; there we used dine together, and practice the ceremonies of our Craft. Ignorant at the time that Masonry was interdicted in Portugal, we made no attempt at secrecy, and were soon denounced by the treacherous zeal of a lady residing in a house opposite to mine, who, at confession declared we were Freemasons; that we debarred women from our assemblies, and, consequently, could be nothing less than dangerous revolutionary conspirators. The officers of the Inquisition were soon on the alert. My friend, Mr. Monton, fell the first victim, he being seized in manner following:

"A jeweler and goldsmith, who besides was familiar of the Holy Office, came to his house, saying he was commissioned to inquire the expense of resetting a diamond weighing four carats. They agreed about the sum; but as this was artifice merely, in order that the familiar might become acquainted with Monton's person, he declined leaving the jewel until after consulting the owner, and hearing his opinion of the arrangement. I happened to be present, which greatly delighted the inquisitor, who had got the unexpected sight of both his victims at once. He went off, requesting both of us to call on him the next day. Business not permitting me to accompany him, Monton went alone to receive the diamond said to be worth a hundred moidores. 'Where is your friend, Coustos,' said the traitor, for he had the day before showed him several stones, which he pretended to be desirous I should polish. Monton replied that I was on change, and he would fetch me. But the inquisitor and his five subordinates, afraid of losing half their prey, beckoned him into the back shop, and after several signs and tokens had passed between him and his myrmidons, he rose up, whispered a few words in private, and retiring behind a curtain, demanded his visitor's name and surname, telling him he was a prisoner in the king's name. Unconscious of any crime for which he could justly incur his Portuguese majesty's displeasure, he gave up his sword the moment it was demanded of him. Finding he had no other weapon, they asked whether he wished to know in whose name he was detained. 'Yes,' said Monton. 'We seize you,' said the guards, 'in the king's name, and in that of the most Holy Inquisition; and in its name we forbid you to speak, or even so much as to murmur.' Then, a door at the bottom of the shop, which looked into a by-lane, flew open, and the prisoner, accompanied by the commissary, was dragged towards a small chaise with the blinds close drawn down, so that were any friends near, they might remain ignorant of his fate.

"The next device was to spread a report that he had absconded with the diamond entrusted to him. How greatly was each of his friends shocked at this slander! As we all esteemed his probity none would give credence to the base report, and we unanimously agreed, after weighing the matter, to go in a body to the jeweler and reimburse him, firmly persuaded that some fatal and unforeseen accident must have led to the disappearance of our friend. He, however, refused our offer, politely assuring us that the owner of the diamond was far too wealthy to be regardful of its loss.

"Truth sometimes penetrates all disguises with which falsehood seeks to cloud her; so this generosity in persons to whom we were in a great measure strangers made us suspect some foul play, a conjecture confirmed by a fierce and open persecution which immediately arose against Freemasonry, I myself being seized four days after.

"An acquaintance, hired by the Inquisition, seeing me in a coffeehouse on the 5th March, 1742, between nine and ten of the clock at night, denounced me to nine familiars, who lay in wait with a chaise near the spot. I was in the utmost confusion when, on quitting the coffeehouse with two friends, they seized me only, 'I had passed my word,' they declared, 'for the diamond which Monton was charged with purloining; therefore certainly I was his accomplice, and had engaged my friends to offer payment in the hope of concealing my crime.'

"To no purpose did I attempt a justification. Seizing my sword the wretches handcuffed me, thrust me into a chaise drawn by two mules, and thus was I hurried off to share the captivity of my friend. But, undaunted by these severities, and their repeated denunciations of vengeance in case I attempted to accost the passersby, I tore open the wooden shutters of my carriage, and loudly hailed one of my friends, Mr. Richard, my companion in the coffeehouse, conjuring them to apprize all our brethren of my imprisonment, and warn them that the only means of averting a similar fate was to go voluntarily to the inquisitors and denounce themselves. Deeds of villainy are deeds of darkness.

"I would here observe that the Holy Office rarely ventures to seize its prey in broad daylight, as in the case of Monton, unless they judge he will be too much paralysed by fear and the, novelty of his position to make either an outcry or resistance. For myself I reckoned so confidently on the zeal and courage of my fiends that my first impulse was to draw and defend myself, calling on my friends to set their backs to the wall and follow my example. No sooner, however, did they see my rapier out than, overwhelmed with terror from being better advised as to the consequences of resistance, they all forsook me and fled. Left alone with these wretches, the whole nine fell upon and pinioned me, as already described. When a person is arrested all the world abandons him. His relatives go into mourning, and scarcely venture to intercede in his defence; nay, steps are taken to bribe and intimidate the dearest friends into accusing each other.

"Swiftly the carriage rattled over the pavement until we reached the Casa Sancta, and swept into a courtyard overshadowed by the dark grey towers of that dreary office. I was now ordered to alight, and handed over to an officer until the grand inquisitor had been informed of my being caught in their snare. They took advantage of this interval to make a rigorous personal search, the rule being to deprive the prisoner of any gold, silver, buckles, knives, etc., which he may have about him. They then motioned me to follow, and led the way to a lone dungeon, expressly forbidding me to speak unless addressed, not to strike against the walls; but in case I wanted assistance to knock at the door with a great padlock that hung outside, and which I could reach by thrusting my arm through the iron grate. 'Twas then that, struck with all the horrors of a place which I had read and heard such baleful descriptions, I sank into the blackest melancholy, picturing to an excited fancy all the pains and penalties that might hereafter be associated with my imprisonment.

"My first day's incarceration passed in these anxious terrors, aggravated by the dismal moans of other captives, my neighbors. And night, usually associated with solemn silence brought no intermission. The shrieks of men and, if I may judge from the voices, of women, undergoing the punishment of scourging for a violation of the command to speak not - so vehemently urged on me - forbid all sleep. I rose to pace my cell. Dawn at length broke through the lofty grated lattice, and full wearily it came. Time seemed no longer to revolve. These twenty-four hours succeeding my capture, had for me the duration of years.

"In three days' time, a lay brother whom I had not yet seen entered my prison, and without one word uttered or sign made, began to crop my hair. Bareheaded, and with naked feet, he then marched me into the presence of my abhorred judges, viz., the president and four junior inquisitors.

"Immediately on my entrance they instructed me to kneel, lay my right hand on the Bible, and swear in the name of Almighty God, that I would truly answer all questions demanded of me. My own and my parents' Christian name and surname, the place of my birth, my profession, religious faith, and how long I had resided at Lisbon, were then entered in a book. This done, the chief inquisitor spoke thus: 'Son you have heinously offended in aspersing the Holy Office, as we know of a certainty. Now, therefore, we exhort you to confession, and to accuse yourself of all and several the crimes committed from the earliest moment at which you could discern betwixt good and evil, to the present hour. Thus doing, you may excite the compassion of our holy tribunal, ever merciful and kind to such as love and speak the truth.'

"They then thought proper to tell me that the diamond transaction mentioned above, was merely a device to gain a convenient opportunity of arresting me. On this, I besought them to let me know the real cause of my imprisonment; that I had never in my life spoken evil of the Romish religion; having so demeaned myself during my sojourn in Lisbon, that I could not be justly accused of saying or doing aught contrary to the laws spiritual or temporal, of his Portuguese majesty's dominions. That I belonged to a society comprising individuals professing various religious tenets, one of whose laws expressly forbade all disputation on matters of doctrine, under a severe penalty. When I perceived the inquisitors confounded the word society with religion, I assured them my society could be considered religious one only as it obliged its members to live in charity and brotherly love, however widely they differed on matters of faith. They then asked how this society was called. I replied that I could tell them its name in English and French, but was unable to translate it into Portuguese. Keenly fixing their eyes on me, they all pronounced alternately the words 'Freemason,' 'Francmacon'. The true cause of my imprisonment was now revealed. After a pause of silence, during which they conferred apart, they suddenly demanded what was the constitution of Freemasonry. I set before them as well as I could our ancient traditions. That James VI of Scotland had declared himself its protector, and encouraged his subjects to enrol themselves therein. That, besides, the ancient kings of Scotland so esteemed this honorable Craft for its devoted loyalty, that they promoted among its members use of a special toast; and 'God preserve the king and brotherhood' precedes the goblet at all their feasts. That those monarchs were often Grand Masters of lodges; when otherwise, a nobleman was selected who received from the king a pension; at his election a money gift from all beside. That Queen Elizabeth ascending the English throne in unsettled times, took umbrage of all secret societies, and resolved to suppress them; but first of all she commanded certain of her council, with the archbishop of Canterbury, to enrol themselves in that of Masonry. Obeying the queen's orders, they made so advantageous a report of their loyalty as removed her Majesty's alarm, and Freemasons have ever since enjoyed in Great Britain and the places subject to it, the most perfect countenance and all due liberty, which it is their proud boast never to have once abused.

"The inquisitors next demanded what was the tendency of this society. I replied: 'Every Freemason is obliged at his admission to take an oath on the Holy Gospel, that he will be faithful to the king, not enter into any plot or conspiracy against his sacred person, or against the liberty of the country where he resides; and that he will cheerfully submit to its established laws. That charity was the foundation, soul, and bond of unity, linking us together by the tie of fraternal love, and making it an imperative duty to assist poverty in the most liberal spirit, without distinction of religious belief.'

"Twas then they called me 'liar,' declaring it to be impossible we should practise these good maxims, and yet be so jealous of our secret as to exclude women from its participation. The judicious reader will smile at the inference, which if true, would certainly apply to the dark and mysterious tyranny of the Holy Office itself. However, I answered them: 'Women, my lords, are excluded in order to suppress occasion of scandal, and because in society they are usually found to be unsafe guardians of a secret. The founders of Masonry are, therefore, by their exclusion, thought to have given a signal proof of their wisdom and foresight.'

"They now insisted I should reveal to them the symbols and tokens of a lodge.

"The oath,' said I, 'taken at my admission, never to divulge directly or indirectly what then transpired, forbids me; and I humbly trust to your lordships' justice that my principles may find favor in your sight.' To this they answered: 'In our presence your heretical vow avails not - we absolve you from it.' The nature of my reply they seemed to anticipate. I was at once thrust back into my damp, noisome dungeon, where I fell sick. Partially recovered, I was sent for to be interrogated whether, since my abode in Lisbon, any Portuguese had been received into a lodge. I replied 'No.' True it was, indeed, that Don Emanuel de Sousa, lord of Calliaris, and captain of the German guards, hearing that the person was at Lisbon who had made the Duc de Villeroy a Freemason by order of the French king, Louis XV, had desired M. de Chavigny, ambassador of France to find me out. But knowing Freemasonry to be forbidden, and aware that M. de Calliaris was a nobleman of great economy, I found an expedient to disengage myself from him by asking fifty moidores for his reception, a demand which, I was persuaded, would at once put an end to his desire to be enrolled amongst us. As regarded their threats of torture I referred them to Mr. Dogood, an English Roman Catholic and Freemason, who had settled a lodge in Lisbon fifteen years before, and who, being of their own persuasion, could more properly appreciate their power to, absolve us from an oath.

"Again referring to a previous examination, when I said it was a duty incumbent on Freemasons to assist the needy, they asked whether I had ever relieved a necessitous object. I named to them a poor woman, a Romanist, who, being reduced to the extremity of want, and hearing that we were liberal of alms, had addressed herself to me: I gave her a gold coin; when the Franciscan convent was burned down the fathers made a collection, and I have them, upon the exchange, three-quarters of a moidore (gold coin); that a poor Roman Catholic, with a large family, who could get no work, being in the utmost distress, had been recommended to me by some Freemasons, with a suggestion that we should make up a purse among ourselves in order to set him up again; accordingly we raised, among seven members, ten moidores, which money I myself put into his hands. They then asked whether I had ever given alms privately out of my own purse. I replied that the above gifts were mainly derived from fines levied at the meetings of the

Brotherhood. 'For what faults?' inquired they. 'Those,' said I, 'who take the sacred name of God in vain pay the quarter of a moidore; less profane oaths or indecent words, the quarter of a new crusade; the fractious and disobedient were also fined.' Finding all their efforts to shake my resolution, either by terror or cajolery, of no avail, they threw off all disguise, called me 'dog of a heretic,' and vowing I was already damned, so that neither purgatory nor absolution would avail me. The proctor then proceeded to read the heads of the indictment or charge, which was as follows:

"The said Coustos having refused to discover to the inquisitors the true tendency and evil designs of the assembly of Freemasons, and having, on the contrary, persisted in the assertion that Freemasonry is good in itself: wherefore the proctor of the Inquisition demands that the said prisoner be prosecuted with the utmost rigor; and that the court do now proceed to tortures, in order to extort from him a confession that the several articles of which he stands accused are wholly and altogether true.'

"Folding up the paper he drove me before him to the torture room, built in the form of a square tower, illuminated by two small torches only, making a darkness visible; and, to prevent the shrieks of the sufferers from being heard without, the doors are lined with felt. After preparing their instruments, an operation ostentatiously performed before my eyes, six wretches laid hold of me, stripping me naked to my drawers, and casting me on my back. An iron collar was placed round my neck and secured me to the scaffold. They next fixed a ring to each foot, and stretched my legs apart with all their might. Afterwards two ropes were twisted round each arm and two round each thigh, and, being passed under the scaffold through holes made for the purpose, four men, upon a signal, suddenly drew them tight. These ropes pierced the flesh, even to my bones, making the blood gush out at the eight different places thus bound. An inquisitor stood by; at each interval in the torture he addressed me. 'Sir,' said he, with a marvellous hypocrisy, in the most anxious and affectionate tone, 'why will you thus endure suffering - why so cruel to yourself? Remember, should you expire under the torture, in the sight of Heaven you are guilty of the crime of *felo de se.*'

"As I persisted in keeping silence, the cords were thus four times drawn together. At my side stood a physician and a surgeon, who, sometimes, feeling my temples or my pulse, directed the tormenters to suspend operations. During these pauses, I lay in a heap upon the ground, until some partial restoration of my faculties, when the tenderhearted inquisitor gave the signal for their repetition.

"Seeing these sufferings elicited no confession - but that the greater the cruelty the more fervently I supplicated heaven for constancy and courage - six weeks after they led me once more to the tower. I was directed to extend my arms with the palms outwards; a rope being attached to each wrist, they turned a windlass, and gradually drew them nearer and nearer to each other behind, until the backs of the hands touched. Both my shoulders were dislocated; from my mouth issued a stream of blood. The operation being thrice repeated, I was taken to my cell, where the surgeon, in setting my bones, put me to almost equal pain.

"At the expiration of two months, being a little restored, a new executioner, clothed in a long black garment which concealed his person from head to foot, with a mask upon his face, having two holes for sight, came to my cell and conducted me to the torture-room. Around my body he placed a heavy iron chain, which crossing upon my stomach, terminated at my wrists. The tormenter stretching these ropes with a roller, pressed and bruised my stomach; and wrists and shoulders were again dislocated. The surgeon, however, set them directly. The sympathizing inquisitor, having repeated his condolence and his exhortations, withdrew, making a sign in doing so for the recommencement of the torture.

"Nine different times they had me on the rack. I was reduced to the state of a helpless cripple, unable during some weeks to raise my hand to my mouth, and my body swelled with inflammation caused by these frequent dislocations. I have too much reason to dread that I shall feel their effects through life, being seized from time to time with thrilling pains, unknown to me else I fell into the bloody hands of these hellish inquisitors.

"The period for a general *auto da fe* being arrived, I was compelled to walk with the other victims. When at St. Dominic's Church, my sentence was read, and I found myself condemned to the galleys for the space of four years.

"There I had leisure to reflect on the means best adapted to obtain my liberty. I succeeded in communicating with my brother-in-law, Mr. Barber, entreating him humbly to address the Earl of Harrington in my favor, as he had the honor to live in his lordship's family. This nobleman, whose humanity and generosity have been the theme of abler pens than mine, undertook to procure my freedom. Accordingly, his lordship spoke to his Grace the Duke of Newcastle, one of the principal secretaries of state, that he would supplicate our sovereign to order his minister at Lisbon to demand me as a British subject. His Majesty, ever attentive to the felicity of his subjects, and desirous to relieve them from all their misfortunes, graciously assented. Instructions were at once sent to Mr. Compton, minister at Lisbon, to demand an immediate audience of the Portuguese minister, and Admiral Matthews, then sailing with a fleet to the Mediterranean, carried these instructions out. His orders were, to anchor for four-and-twenty hours only in the Tagus, and within half that period to see me safely delivered on board some English vessel about to sail for England. The tenor of this dispatch was too significant to be dallied with. An order came for my immediate release, and I left the prison of the galleys on the 25th October, 1743.

"I return our sovereign, King George II, my most dutiful acknowledgments for having graciously condescended to interpose in behalf of an unhappy galley-slave. I shall retain as long as I have health, the deepest affection and loyalty for his sacred person, and shall be ever ready to expose my life, as every true-hearted Freemason is bound to do, for his Majesty and all his august family."

The year following the celebrated auto-da-fe at Lisbon - in July, 1844 - another Freemason, a friend of Coustos, John Baptist Richard, 26 years of age, who had been denounced as a Freemason, renounced the Protestant religion in order to regain his liberty, which he succeeded in doing on payment of the costs of the prosecution. Among the names of those denounced to the Inquisition at this time were Englishmen named Gordon, Fox, Ivens, Vandrevel; Frenchmen named Jean Pietre, Lambert Boulanger, Jean Ville Neuve, Felix, Julian, and Carmoa. Gordon and Fox were already initiated when they went to Portugal, and it may be that this Gordon is the same as the brother indicated by O'Kelly as having introduced Freemasonry into Portugal.

It is not without interest to note the way in which the authorities first discovered the fact that Coustos and Monton were Freemasons. It appears that Monton's wife, in conversation with a Mme. la Rude, the wife of the Jeweller, was so indiscreet as to reveal the fact that her husband was a Freemason. Mme. la Rude, who was jealous of the property of her two friends, made this known to another friend, Marie Rose Clave, with the result that Monton, Coustos, and another Freemason, a Frenchman named Brusle, were arrested. Several foreigners were members of the lodge of which Coustos was Master, but, when interrogated, they denied their membership.

It seems almost if not quite, incredible that such things could have happened within the last two hundred years, but the narrative of Coustos was verified at the time it was written, and there is no reason to suspect as untrue or exaggerated any one of the statement he has and, Monton returned with Coustos to London where both were well cared for by the English brethren. His narrative, together with a history of the Inquisition, was published in 1745, and again in 1746. There is a copy of the very rare first edition in the Bodleian Library.

Chapter II

IN THE YEAR following the release of Coustos - 1744 - the Madrid Inquisition tribunal sentenced to *abjuration de levi* and banishment from Spain, Don Francisco Aurion de Roscobel, Canon of Quintanar, for membership of the Freemasons.

A Papal Bull to be operative in any country must be published in that country, and this not having been done in Switzerland, the papal bulls had no locus standi or authority there, but, in 1745, an astonishing edict was promulgated by the Council of Berne. It was worded as follows:

"We, the Advoyer, the little and great council of the city and republic of Berne, make known to all men by these presents: Having learnt that a certain societies named Freemasons, spreads itself every day more and more into all the cities and towns under our government, and that the persons who have joined the said society are received under various solemn engagements, and even by oath: Wherefore, having seriously reflected upon the consequences thereof and considered that such meetings and associations are directly contrary to the fundamental laws and constitutions of our country, and, in particular, to the protection required on our part to discountenance any assemblies under our government, without our knowledge and express permission: Moreover, it has appeared to us, that if an effectual remedy was not immediately taken, the consequence of that neglect might be dangerous to the State; For these reasons, and through our paternal affection as much for the public good and private advantage of all our citizens and subjects, we have found it absolutely necessary to dissolve and totally abolish the said society, which we do by these presents; and henceforth, for ever, we forbid, annul, and abolish in all our territories and districts, to all persons that now are or shall hereafter come under our dominions; and we do, in the first place ordain and decree, that all those, our citizens and subjects, who are actually known to be Freemasons, shall be obliged immediately to adjure by oath the engagements they have taken in the said society, before the bailiff or officer of the district where they live, without delay. And as to our citizens and subjects who actually are Freemasons, and not publicly known to be such, and who, nevertheless, at present reside in our dominions, or may hereafter came under our obedience, our sovereign will and pleasure is, that those who shall be found in our dominions, shall be bound to renounce their obligation in the space of one month from the date hereof: and those who are absent must submit to the same terms, to be reckoned from the date of their return, not only to accuse themselves, but to adjure and renounce their engagements, those who present themselves in our capital city, to the reigning Advoyer and in other cities, and in the country, to the bailiff of the place; and from them they shall receive assurance of safety to their persons, if they abjure and renounce their obligations without delay, in the same form as all other Masons are obliged to do.

"Upon failure in any part hereof, they shall all undergo the punishment hereafter declared. But to the end that no person shall dare, for the time to come, to entice, tempt, solicit, or be so enticed, tempted, or solicited, to engage him or themselves, into this same society of Freemasons, we have thought fit to ordain and decree as follows:

"That all those Masons who shall hold their assemblies in our dominions, or entice, tempt, or solicit others into their associations, as well as all our citizens and subjects in our dominions, and elsewhere, as also those who have been set at liberty, shall for the future frequent such assemblies, they shall all and every one of them be subjected to the fine of one hundred crowns, without remission; and likewise be deprived of whatever place, trust, benefit, or employment he shall now hold; and if they have no present employment or office, shall be rendered incapable of holding such for the time to come.

"And touching the place or lodge where these kind of assemblies are held for the future, the person or persons who shall let or furnish them with the house, room, or place, for the holding of such lodge, shall be subjected to the same fine of one hundred crowns; one- third of which to the informer, one-third to the bailiff of the place, and one-third to the hospitals, or fund of the poor, where such assemblage shall be held. Let it be well understood that all offenders who shall leave our dominions, in order to avoid the payment of the said fine, shall be banished from our dominions for ever, or till they shall have paid it, upon pain of death. We moreover reserve at pleasure, to punish with more or less vigor, according to the case of the person so rendering himself up to our sovereign pleasure, or those who, notwithstanding their abjuration, shall have again entered into the society, or frequent any of their assemblies.

"We do finally ordain and command, that all our bailiffs and ministers of justice do cause these presents to be published in all churches, and to be affixed up in the accustomed places, and see that these our commands are strictly and faithfully executed.

"Given in our Great Council the 3rd of March, 1745."

In the same year the Town Council of Geneva renewed an edict against the Craft which it had issued in the previous year, but of which no one had taken any notice. The second edict appears also to have had little effect, for lodges were continually being formed in Geneva though they do not seem to have been permanent until 1768, when the Lodge of Hearts, the first in Geneva to keep a Minute Book, was founded. Although there was in France, in 1748, a discussion among the Roman Catholic clergy as to whether a parishioner who was a Freemason should be permitted to receive the Sacraments, when six doctors of the Sorbonne passed some resolutions which declared Freemasonry to be pernicious and bad, the Parlement of Paris refused to register the Bull of Clement XII, and when, in 1750, the Jubilee attracted crowds of pilgrims to Rome, so many had to seek that relief on 18th May, 1751, Benedict XIV was led to revive the Masonic prohibition in his Bull Provides.

The wording of that Bull was as follows:

"Wherein some Societies or Conventicles of Liberi Muratori, or Freemasons, or however else named, are again condemned and prohibited.

"Benedict, Bishop, Servant of the Servants of God. For the permanent record of the matter.

"The prudent laws of our predecessors, the Roman Pontiffs, the vigor of which we fear may either by lapse of time or neglect of man be weakened or destroyed and that they may have fresh force and full strength, and we think there is just and weighty cause for their need of strengthening and confirming by the fresh fortification of our authority.

"It is true that our predecessor of happy memory, Pope Clement XII, by his Apostolic Letter, dated 28th April, 1738, in the eighth year of his Pontificate, inscribed to all the faithful in Christ, commencing with the words In Eminenti, condemned in perpetuity and prohibited all such societies, meetings, gatherings, clubs, conventicles, or clubs known as Liberi Muratori, or Freemasons, then widely distributed in various parts, and growing in strength daily, instructing the faithful in Christ, all and singly, under pain of excommunication, from which no one could be absolved by any other than the Roman Pontiff for the time being, except at the hour of death, and that none should dare or presume to enter societies of this kind, or to propagate, foster, admit, or conceal them, or be enrolled in them, or take part in their proceedings, and much more to the same effect as may be seen from the Letter which was as follows."

Then followed in extenso the Bull of Clement XII, as given on Roman Catholicism and Freemasonry part 2. After this recapitulation, Pope Benedict XIV proceeded:

"Since, however, as we have heard, there have been some who have not hesitated to assert and openly contend that the aforesaid penalty of excommunication imposed by our predecessor, as set forth above, is no longer effective because the preceding Constitution has not been confirmed by us, as though the express confirmation of a pontifical successor is required for the subsistence of Apostolic Constitutions issued by predecessors

"And since also it has been suggested to us some pious and God-fearing men that with the object of doing away with all quibbling and subterfuge of quibblers, that we should declare the agreement of our mind and will with that of our predecessor, and they regard it as highly expedient to add the support of our confirmation to the Constitution of our predecessor:

"We, although up to the present, whilst we have conceded absolution to many faithful in Christ who were truly penitent and contrite at having violated the terms of the same Constitution, and who sincerely promised that they would wholly withdraw from the condemned Societies or Conventicles, and never afterwards return to them, both before and especially in Jubilee year which has just elapsed, and whilst we have granted faculties to Penitentiaries deputed by us, enabling them in our name and authority to grant the like absolution to penitents of the same class who applied to them; whilst also with anxious zeal and vigilance we have not failed to urge that proceedings should be taken in accordance with the measure their offence against the violators of the same Constitution, by competent judges and tribunals - a service, in fact, often rendered - although we have thus given plain and unquestioned proofs of our sentiments, of our firm and deliberate will as regards the force subsistence of the censure imposed by our said predecessor, Pope Clement XII, from which our opinion ought quite plainly to have been inferred: and if a contrary opinion of us were circulated we might regard with indifference and contempt and leave our judgment in the hands of Almighty God, making use of the words which, as is well known, were recited formerly during sacred actions: 'Grant, Lord, we pray Thee, that we may not regard the abuse of reprobate liars, but, trampling underfoot the same wickedness, we implore Thee to suffer us not to be terrified by their abuse, neither entangled by their treacherous flatteries.' Thus stands in our ancient Missal, which is ascribed to St. Gelasius, our predecessor, and which was published that Venerable Servant of God, Joseph Maria Cardinal Thomas, in the Mass entitled: 'Against them who speak against us.' "Howsoever, lest anything unwittingly omitted us might seem to have weight, and with the object of doing away with such false calumny and stopping the same, after hearing the counsel of some Venerable brethren of the Holy Roman Church, we have decided on the confirmation by the present document of the same Constitution as our predecessor, as above, inserting word for word, in the specific form held to be the amplest and most effective. Accordingly, from certain knowledge, and in the plentitude of our Apostolic authority, by the tenor of these presents, in everything and throughout, exactly as if it had first been published in our own motion and authority and name, we confirm, corroborate, and renew it and will it to have perpetual force and efficacy, and do so decree.

"Furthermore, among the gravest causes of the before mentioned prohibition and condemnation set forth in the Constitution inserted above, one is that men of every religion and sect are associated together in the societies and conventicles of this character; from which circumstance it is obvious how great an injury may be inflicted on the purity of the (Roman) Catholic Religion; a second is the close and impenetrable bond of secrecy whereby the proceedings of such Conventicles are kept hidden, to which may deservedly be applied the sentiment expressed by Caecilius Natalis in Minucius Felix, in a very different cause: 'Things honorable always delight in publicity: crimes are secret.' A third is the oath whereby the members bind themselves to keep a secret of the kind inviolably; as though it where lawful for anyone under pretext of any promise or oath, to protect himself from being bound to confess, when questioned by legitimate authority, all that is demanded for the purpose of ascertaining whether anything is done in Conventicles of this character contrary to the existence of religion, the state, and the laws. A fourth is that Societies of this description are known to be in opposition to civil no less than canonical sanctions, for it is well known that by Civil Law all Colleges and Sodalities are prohibited if formed irrespective of public authority, as may be seen in the 47th Book of the Pandects, Tit. 22: 'On Unlawful Colleges and Corporations,' and in the well-known epistle of Caius Plinius Secundus, Book X, 87, in which he says that, by his edict, in accordance with the mandate of the Emperor, the formation of Heteriae was forbidden, that is to say, the formation and holding of Societies and Conventicles without the authority of the Prince. A fifth is that already in many quarters the said Societies and Meetings have been banished and proscribed by the laws made by secular princes. Lastly, because these same Societies were of ill repute among wise and virtuous men, and, in their judgment, all who joined them incurred the brand of depravity and perversion.

"Our same predecessor, in concluding the above inserted Constitution, calls on the Bishops, higher Prelates, and other local Ordinaries not to omit, for its due execution, if need be the invocation of the secular arm.

"These injunctions, all and singly, are not only approved and confirmed by us and commended and enjoined on the same Ecclesiastical Superiors, but we ourselves also in accordance with our duty of Apostolic solicitude, by our present letters, invoke the aid of all secular powers and their assistance in carrying into effect the measures above set forth, and we most urgently demand it, since the Sovereign Princes and Powers have been chosen by God to be Defenders of the Faith and Protectors of the Church; and since it is their duty by all reasonable means to show the obedience due to the Apostolic Constitutions, and the fullest observance of them; whereof they have been reminded by the Fathers of the Council of Trent, Session xxv, cap. 20, long before in the excellent declaration of the Emperor Charlemagne in Tit. 1, C. 2, of his Capitularies, where, after demanding from all his subjects observance of Ecclesiastical Sanctions, he adds: 'For we can in no way recognize how men can be faithful to us who have shewn themselves disobedient to their own priests, and unfaithful to God.' Wherefore, enjoining on all ministers and agents of government absolutely to enforce due obedience to the laws of the Church, he announced the severest penalty against those who neglected to grant it adding, amongst other things: 'But, whoever amongst them (which God forbid) shall neglect and be disobedient to these laws, let them know that they neither continue to hold office in our Empire, even though they should be our own children, nor have place in the Palace, nor keep company nor any communication with us and ours, but rather shall they undergo punishment in solitude and wretchedness.'

"Further, we will that the same credit be given to copies of these presents, under the subscription of some Public Notary and guaranteed by the Seal of a Person of Ecclestical Dignity, exactly as would have been given to the original letter if produced and exhibited.

"Let no man, therefore, regard it as lawful to infringe or with rash daring contravene this document of our confirmation, renewal, approval, charge, appeal, requisition, decree, and will. And if anyone presume to attempt this, let him know that he will incur the wrath of Almighty God, of Saints Peter and Paul, and of the Apostles.

"Dated from Rome, St. Mary the Greater, A. D. 1751, 18th May, in the 11th year of our Pontificate." (Signed)

"Registered in the Secretariat of the Briefs, A. D., 18th May, in the 11th year of the Pontificate of the Most Holy in Christ, our Father and Lord Benedict XIV, by Divine Providence Pope. Accordingly, the above mentioned Constitution was affixed and published on the doors of the Lateran Basilica, and of the

Chief of the Apostles, and in other customary and usual places by me, Francis Bartolotti, Apostolic Pursuivant."

The Bull was published in various dioceses, though not throughout the Catholic world, and, therefore, was only partially operative, and did not call for universal obedience among Roman Catholics, for, as already stated, a Bull only becomes operative in its Provisions and demands and obligations when and where published.

When the Bull was published in a diocese it was always accompanied with a letter from the Archbishop or Bishop. The following copy of the Ordinance issued by the Archbishop of Avignon may be taken as a sample of these communications:

"Ordinance for the publication of the Bull of our Holy Father Pope Benedict XIV, which condemns and forbids anew the Societies of so-called Freemasons, invoking the arm and aid of Princes and secular Powers.

"JOSEPH DE GUYON DE CROCHANS, by the grace of God and of the Apostolic See, Archbishop of Avignon.

"TO THE CLERGY, Secular and Regular, and to all the Faithful of our diocese, Greeting and Benediction in our Lord Jesus Christ.

"We have long lamented, my very dear brethren, in the privacy of our heart, the surprising blindness of some amongst you who allowing themselves to be seduced by the artifices of the Devil, and giving way to the deceptive zest for unhappy novelty, rashly engage in the Societies of so-called Freemasons, and persist obstinately in so doing, in spite of the prohibition which has been issued by the Apostolic See under the most terrible of ecclesiastical penalties, Major Excommunication reserved for the Supreme Pontiff.

"The sacred Jubilee, which appears to have revived the faith and religion nearly extinct in many among you, causing a cessation of secret assemblies of these suspected associations, had raised the hope in us that we had happily seen the end of them among our flock. The Constitution which our Holy Father Pope Benedict XIV, happily reigning, has just published against these same Societies will, as we hope, destroy them entirely and crown our righteous desires.

"We hasten, my very dear brethren, to acquaint you with this Bull, so worthy of its author: you will see in it fresh marks of the zeal and wisdom of this great Pontiff whom the Christian universe does not cease to admire, you will see in it the solemn confirmation of the Bull which his predecessor, Pope Clement XII, of happy memory, had promulgated in the year 1738 against the Societies of so-called Freemasons, and those among you who may still be of that number, cannot avoid being seriously alarmed at having merited the thunders of the Church.

"For this it is necessary to give you a precis of the contents of the Bulls of these great Popes. They concur unanimously in overwhelming you with the weight of their authority if you have the misfortune to continue still in Societies solemnly condemned by the Vicar of Jesus Christ.

"It is, then, in virtue of holy obedience, that the successor of the Apostle Peter lays strict commands on all and each of the Faithful, of whatever age, rank, condition, order, dignity, and preeminence, be they laics, be they clerics, be they seculars, be they regulars, though they might claim to have express and individual mention made of them, that none of them under any color or pretext whatever, venture or presume to introduce, adhere to, and maintain the Societies of so-called Freemasons, or by whatever name they are called; or to receive and shelter them in their houses or elsewhere; or to engage in them, associate in them, be present at them; or to give permission or facility for assembling there; or to provide them with anything, or to give them advice, help, or favor in any matter whatever, of oneself or through another, directly or indirectly in public or in private; or to exhort, induce, and encourage others to enrol themselves in these Societies, or to persuade them to join them, be present at them, or to help and support them in any manner; but that they shall be bound to keep wholly aloof from these Societies, Aggregations, Companies, and Conventicies under pain of Excommunication, incurred by the mere fact, without there being need of formal notice; from which there can be no absolution, except on the point of death, unless by the Supreme Pontiff.

"The reasons for a prohibition and condemnation so express, which His Holiness is graciously pleased to state in his Bull are worthy of his wisdom, and well fitted to induce you to renounce altogether practices the improprieties and dangers of which they so earnestly set forth.

"The first of these reasons is that from men of every kind of religion and sect uniting together, and binding one another in these Societies and Assemblies, the purity of the (Roman) Catholic religion, the sole verity, cannot but suffer, sooner or later, great injury.

"The second is the strict law of impenetrable secrecy under which all that goes on in such assemblies is carefully concealed.

"The third is the oath by which one engages to keep the secret inviolably, as though it were permitted under any pretext of promise or oath whatever to shield oneself from making complete avowal when interrogated by lawful authority in order to ascertain whether anything is done in their assemblies that may be contrary to Religion or State.

"The fourth is that Societies of this kind are not less opposed to Civil Laws than to the Canonical and Ecclesiastical Ordinances, the Civil Law prohibiting Societies which are formed without public authority.

"The fifth is that these Societies and these Conventicles have already been proscribed and banished from several states by the authority of Secular Princes.

"Finally, the last of these reasons is that these same Associations and Assemblies are thought ill of by the wise and virtuous, and that in their judgment whoever connects himself with them, gives occasion to suspect him of irregularity and disorder.

"Pope Clement XII, in his Constitution of 1738, had ordered Bishops, Higher Prelates, and other local Ordinaries, as well as the Inquisitors of the Faith, to seek out diligently violators of the Constitution, to proceed against them, of whatever age, rank, condition, order, dignity, and preeminence they were, and to punish them with suitable penalties, as being strongly suspected of heresy, giving with that object free power to invoke, if necessary, the aid of the secular arm. His Holiness renews to us today the command of his predecessor and as a result of his Apostolic solicitude, he urgently invokes the aid and support of Catholic Princes, for the execution of his Bull in their dominions; he tells them they are set by God to be defenders of the Faith, and Protectors of the Church, and to animate their zeal to fulfil these glorious functions. His Holiness reminds them of these beautiful words of the pious Emperor Charlemagne in the first Tit of his Capitularies, Ch. 2: 'We cannot possibly recognize as faithful to us those who show themselves unfaithful to God and to their priests.'

"Such, my very dear brethren, is the ardent zeal which our Holy Father the Pope exhibited for the destruction of the societies and Assemblies of Freemasons.

"For these reasons, in pursuance of the intentions and orders of His Holiness, and in execution of his Bull, we order that it be published at the altar of each parish of this city, and that all, those who are engaged in the Societies or Assemblies of these so- called Freemasons, or called by whatever name, withdraw from them altogether, and for ever renounce them with true repentance for having ever taken part in them, that for this purpose they address themselves to Us or to the Reverend Father Inquisitor, or to one of our Vicars General, that they furnish absolutely unequivocal marks of their perfect obedience to the voice of the Vicar of Jesus Christ, and that they put themselves in a state to profit by the grace of the Jubilee just expiring, to receive absolution from the Excommunication reserved for the Holy See, which they have unhappily incurred.

"And since we cannot be ignorant that there is in this city a book in manuscript containing the rules of these Societies of so-called Freemasons, as well as the signatures of those who have joined them, we strictly command, under penalty of Excommunication, that it be given unreservedly into our hands, or those of the Reverend Father Inquisitor; and we likewise command under the same penalty those who know where the book is, without delay, to inform us or the Reverend Father Inquisitor, or one of our Vicars-General.

"If anyone, which God forbid, is so blind and hardened as to continue still in these Societies of so-called Freemasons, or called by another name, let him know that we will proceed against him with the utmost rigor of the Law.

"And this our present Command shall be read and published at the altars of the Parishes, and in all the Communities of men, Secular and Regular, and affixed to the doors of the Metropolitan Church, and of the Parish Churches.

"Given at Avignon in our Archiepiscopal Palace, July 22nd, 1751.

(Signed) Joseph, Archbishop of Avignon, "per Monseigneur Philip, Secretary."

It may be explained that the term "Regular" is applied to a cleric member of any of the Religious Orders or Congregations, and the term "Secular" to one who is in holy orders, but not a member of any Religious Order or Congregation.

It has been stated by some writers that the Pope was instigated to issue this Bull by the solicitations of the King of Naples and others because, being himself a Freemason, having been initiated into the Order some years previously, he might, by such means, stifle suspicion and calm the minds of the bigoted, ignorant, and weak.

Bower says that Benedict XIV was a man of untainted character, of extraordinary parts, and in every respect worthy of and equal to so high a station. He undertook in the very beginning the Herculean labor of cleansing the Church as well as the court, and extirpating the many crying abuses that had taken deep root in both. But his diminishing the number of festivals, his abolishing some vain and senseless ceremonies, his dislike of the grosser superstitions that prevailed in the Church, and his undisguised disapprobation of the many pious, or rather, impious, frauds, countenanced or connived at by his predecessors, gave great offence to sone bigoted Cardinals and procured for him the odious denomination of the Protestant Pope from the deluded multitude. He was a generous and munificent encourager of learning and himself a most learned writer."

One immediate result of the publication of this Bull was that the Order was reanimated in Naples and the members of the Fraternity became more numerous and zealous than ever before. At first, however, Charles III of Naples, influenced by the Bull, prohibited Freemasonry throughout his dominions, but so soon changed his views that in the following year - 1752 - he entrusted his son's education to a Freemason and priest, whom he also appointed to be his own confessor.

The Bull of Benedict XIV gave fresh courage to the clergy surrounding the Austrian throne, and renewed efforts to suppress Freemasonry were made. The Empress, however, although she is said to have been bitterly opposed to the Craft, held her hand and it is stated, with some show of authority, that she visited a lodge in company with one of her ladies, both disguised as men, in order to assure herself that none of the fair sex were admitted to the Order. Having satisfied herself on this point she retired.

In Spain, Fernando VI, immediately on the publication of the Bull, issued a *pragmatica* in which he forbade the formation of lodges under pain of the royal indignation and punishment: all judges were required to report delinquents and all commanders of armies and fleets to dismiss with dishonor any culprits discovered in the service. One Tournon, a Frenchman, resident in Spain, was convicted of practising the rites of Freemasonry and after a tedious confinement in the dungeons of the Inquisition, was finally banished from the kingdom. On the 2nd of July, 1751, Father Joseph Torrubia, a member of the Inquisition, obtained from Ferdinand - VI a decree condemning Freemasons to death without the benefits of a trial of any kind. It is stated that he traitorously caused himself to be initiated into the Order so that he might be in a position to betray the members of the Inquisition. There is a report of his still extant which mentions that there were at that time no fewer than ninety-seven lodges in Spain.

CHAPTER III

L. LORENTE, the author of the *History of the Inquisition*, who was himself secretary of one of the Inquisition tribunals, canon of the Primatical Church of Toledo, Chancellor of the University of that city, Knight of the Order of Charles III, and member of the Royal Academies of History and of the Spanish Language at Madrid, has left on record the following lengthy statement concerning M. Tournon's appearance before the Inquisitors.. He says:

"M. Tournon, a Frenchman, had been invited into Spain and pensioned by the government in order to establish a manufactory of brass or copper buckles and to instruct Spanish workmen. On 30th April, 1757, he was denounced to the Holy Office as suspected of heresy by one of his pupils, who acted in obedience to the commands of his confessor.

"The charges were: (1), That M. Tournon had asked his pupils to become Freemasons, promising that the Grand Orient of Paris should send a Commission to receive them into the Order, if they should submit to the trials he should propose, to ascertain their courage and firmness; and that their titles of reception should be expedited from Paris; (2), that some of these young workmen appeared inclined to comply if M. Tournon would inform them of the object of the Institution. That, in order to satisfy them, he told them severally extraordinary things, and showed them a sort of picture on which were figured instruments of architecture and astronomy. They thought that these representations related to sorcery and they were confirmed in the idea on hearing the imprecations, which M. Tournon said were to accompany the oath of secrecy.

"It appeared from the depositions of three witnesses that M. Tournon was a Freemason. He was arrested and imprisoned on 20th May, 1757, at Madrid, The following conversation which took place in the first audience of monition, is of interest. After asking his name, birthplace, and his reasons for coming to Spain, and making him swear to speak the truth, the Inquisitor proceeded:

"Q. Do you know or suppose why you have been arrested by the Holy Office?

"A. I suppose it is for having said that I was a Freemason.

"Q. Why do you suppose that?

"A. Because I have informed my pupils that I was of that Order, and I fear they have denounced me, for I have perceived lately that they speak to me with an air of mystery, and their questions lead me to believe that they think me a heretic.

"Q. Did you tell them the truth?

"A. Yes.

"Q. You are then a Freemason?

"A. Yes.

"Q. How long have you been so?

"A. For twenty years.

"Q. Have you attended the assemblies of Freemasons?

"A. Yes, at Paris.

"Q. Have you attended them in Spain?

"A. No. I do not know if there are any lodges in Spain.

"Q. If there were, would you attend them?.

"A. Yes.

"Q. Are you a Christian, a Roman Catholic?

"A. Yes, I was baptized in the parish of St. Paul, at Paris

"Q. How, as a Christian, can you dare to attend Masonic assemblies, when you know, or ought to know, that they are contrary to religion?

"A. I do not know that; I am ignorant of it at present, because I never saw or heard anything there which was contrary to religion.

"Q. How can you say that, when you know that Freemasons profess indifference in matters of religion, which is contrary to the Article of Faith which teaches us that no man can be saved who does not profess the Catholic, Apostolic, and Roman religion?

"A. Freemasons do not profess that indifference. But it is indifferent if the person received into the Order be a Catholic or not.

"Q. Then the Freemasons are an anti-religious body?

"A. That cannot be, for the object of the Institution is not to combat or deny any religion, but for the exercise of charity towards the unfortunate of any sect, particularly if he is a member of the Society.

"Q. We prove that indifference is the religious character of Freemasons, that they do not acknowledge the Holy Trinity, since they only confess one God, whom they call T.G.A.O.T.U., which agrees with the doctrine of heretical Philosophies, who say that there is no true religion but only religion, in which the existence of God, the Creator only is allowed, and the rest considered as a human invention. And as M. Tournon has professed himself to be the Catholic religion he is required by the respect he owes to our Saviour, Jesus Christ, true God and true man, and to His Blessed Mother, the Virgin Mary, our Lady, to declare the truth according to his oath, because, in that case, he will acquit his conscience, and it will be allowable to treat him with that mercy and compassion which the Holy Office always shows towards sinners who confess; and if, on the contrary, he conceals anything he will be punished with all the severity of justice, according to the holy Canons of the laws of the kingdom.

"A. The mystery of the Holy Trinity is neither maintained nor combatted in the Masonic lodges; neither is the religious system of the natural philosophies approved or rejected. God is designated as T. G. A. O. T. U., according to the allegories of the Freemasons, which relate to architecture. In order to fulfil my promise of speaking the truth, I must repeat that, in Masonic lodges, nothing takes place which concerns any religious system, and that the subjects treated of are foreign to religion, under the allegories of architectural works.

"Q. Do you believe, as a Catholic, that it is a sign of superstition to mingle holy and religious things with profane things ?

"A. I am not sufficiently acquainted with the particular things which are proscribed as contrary to the purity of the 'Christian religion; but I have believed till now that those who confound the one with the other either by mistake or a vain belief, are guilty of the sin of superstition.

"Q. Is it true that in the ceremonies which accompany the reception of a Mason, the crucified image of our Saviour, the corpse of a man, and a skull, and other objects of a profane nature, are made use of ?

"A. The general statutes of Freemasonry do not ordain these things: if they are made use of, it must have arisen from a particular custom, or from the arbitrary regulations of the members of the body, who are commissioned to prepare for the receptions of candidates; for each lodge had particular customs and ceremonies.

"Q. That is not the question; say if it is true that these ceremonies are observed in Masonic lodges.

"A. Yes, or no, according to the requirements of those who are charged with the ceremonies of initiation.

"Q. Were they observed when you were initiated?

"A. No.

"Q. What oath is necessary to take on being received a Freemason?

"A. We swear to observe secrecy.

"Q. On what?

"A. On things which it may be inconvenient to publish.

"Q. Is this oath accompanied by execrations?

"A. Yes.

"Q. What are they? "

"A. We consent to suffer all the evils which can afflict the body and soul if we violate, the oath.

"Q. Of what importance is this oath, since it is believed that such formidable execrations may be used without indecency?

"A. That of good order in the Society.

"Q. What passes in these lodges which it might be inconvenient to publish?

"A. Nothing, if it is looked upon without prejudice; but as people are generally mistaken in this matter, it is necessary to avoid giving cause for malicious interpretations; and this would take place if what passes when the brethren assemble was made public.

"Q. Of what use is the crucifix, if the reception of a Freemason is not considered a religious act?

"A. It is presented to penetrate the soul with the most profound respect at the moment that the novice takes the oath. It is not used in every lodge and only when particular grades are conferred.

"Q. Why is the skull used?

"A. "That the idea of death may inspire a horror of perjury.

"Q. Of what use is the corpse?

"A. To complete the allegory of Hiram, architect of the temple of Jerusalem; who, it is said, was assassinated by traitors, and to induce a greater detestation of assassination and every offence against our neighbors, to whom we ought to be as benevolent brothers.

"Q. Is it true that the festival of St. John is celebrated in the lodges, and that Masons have chosen him for their patron?

"A. Yes.

"Q. What worship is rendered him in celebrating his festival?

"A. None; that it may not be mingled with profane things. This celebration is confined to a fraternal repast, after which a discourse is read, exhorting the guests to beneficence towards their fellow creatures, in honor of God, the Great Architect, Creator, and Preserver of the Universe.

"Q. Is it true that the sun, moon, and stars are honored in the lodges?

"A. No.

"Q. Is it true that their images or symbols are exposed?

"A. Yes.

"Q. Why are they used?

"A. In order to elucidate the allegories of the great, continual, and true light which the lodges receive from the Great Architect of the world, and these representations belong to the brethren, and encourage them to be charitable.

"Q. M. Tournon will observe that all the explanations he has given of the facts and ceremonies which take place in the lodges are false and different from those which he voluntarily communicated to other persons worthy of belief; he is, however, again invited by the respect he owes to God and the Holy Virgin to declare and confess the heresies of indifferentism, the errors of superstition which mingle holy and profane things, and the errors of idolatry which led him to worship the stars: this confession is necessary for the acquittal of his conscience and the good of his soul; because if he confesses with sorrow for having committed these crimes, detesting them and humbly soliciting pardon (before the fiscal accuses him of these heinous sins) the holy tribunal will be permitted to exercise towards him that compassion and mercy which it always displays to repentant sinners; and because he is judicially accused, he must be treated with all the severity prescribed against heretics by the holy canons, apostolic bulls and the laws of the kingdom.

"A. I have declared the truth and if any witnesses have deposed to the contrary, they have mistaken the meaning of my words, for I have never spoken on this subject to any but the workmen in my manufactory, and then only in the same sense convey by my replies.

"Q. Not content with being a Freemason, you have persuaded other persons to be received into the Order, and to embrace the heretical pursuits and pagan errors into which you have fallen.

"A. It is true that I have requested these persons to become Freemasons, because I thought it would be useful to them if they travelled into foreign countries, where they might meet brethren of their Order who could assist them in any difficulty; but it is not true that I encouraged them to adopt any errors contrary to the Catholic faith, since no such errors are to found in Freemasonry, which does not concern any points of doctrine.

"Q. It has been already proved that these are not chimerical; therefore let M. Tournon consider that he has been a dogmatizing heretic, and that it is necessary that he should acknowledge it with humility, and ask pardon and absolution for the censures which he has incurred; since if he persists in his obstinacy he will destroy both his body and soul; and as this is the first audience of monition he is advised to reflect on his condition, and prepare for the two other audiences which are granted by the compassion and mercy which the holy tribunal always feels for the accused."

M. Tournon was taken back to the prison and persisted in giving the same answers in the two remaining audiences. When brought before the court when the fiscal presented his act of accusation he confessed facts but explained them as he had done before. He refused to choose an advocate on the ground that Spanish lawyers were not acquainted with the Masonic lodges and were as much prejudiced against them as the public. He therefore thought it better to acknowledge that to was wrong and might have been deceived from being ignorant of particular doctrines; he demanded absolution and offered to perform any penance that might be imposed on him, adding that he hoped the punishment would be moderate on account of the good faith which he had shown and which he always preserved, seeing nothing but beneficence practised and recommended in the Masonic lodges without denying or combatting any article of the Roman Catholic faith.

He was condemned to be imprisoned for one year after which he was to be conducted under an escort the frontiers of France; he was banished from Spain forever, unless he obtained permission to return from the King or the Holy Office. He also signed his abjuration with a promise never a again to attend the assemblies of the Freemasons. He went to France at the termination of his imprisonment and it does not appear that he ever returned to Spain.

In the same year that the foregoing occurred - 1757 - the Associate Synod of Scotland attempted to disturb the peace of the Fraternity. Happily, these bigoted dissenters did not possess a fraction of the power of the Church of Rome, or of the Council of Berne, but their proceedings were prompted by a like fanaticism, and would have been marked with the same severity, but, fortunately for the Order, their power extended only to the spiritual concerns of those delinquents who were of the same sect as themselves. At the beginning of 1745 a complaint was lodged before the Synod of Stirling stating that many improper things were performed at the initiation of Freemasons and requesting that the Synod would consider whether or not the members of that Order were entitled to partake of the ordinances of religion. The Synod referred the matter to the Kirk Sessions under their inspection, allowing them to act as they thought proper. In 1755, they ordered that every person who was suspected of being a Freemason should return an explicit answer to any question that might be asked concerning the Masonic oath. In the course of these examinations the Kirk Sessions discovered (for they seem hitherto to have been ignorant of it) that men who were not architects were admitted into the Order. On this account the Synod, in the year 1757, thought it necessary to adopt stricter measures. They drew up a list of foolish questions, which they commanded every Kirk Session to put to those under their charge. These questions related to what they thought were the ceremonies of Freemasonry and those who refused to answer them were debarred from religious ordinances. The Act of the Associate Synod was in the following terms:

"Whereas the oath is one of the most solemn acts of religious worship, which ought to be taken only upon important and necessary occasions; and to be sworn in truth, in judgment and in righteousness, without any mixture of sinful, profane, or superstitious devices:

"And, whereas the Synod had laid before them, in their meeting at Stirling on the 17th March, 1745, an overture concerning the Mason oath, bearing that there were very strong presumptions that among Masons an oath of secrecy is administered to entrants into their Society, even under a capital penalty, and before any of these things which they swear to keep secret be revealed to them; and that they pretend to take some of these secrets from the Bible; beside other things which are ground on scruple, in the manner of swearing the said oath; and therefore overturning, that the Synod would consider the whole affair, and give directions with respect to the admission of persons engaged in that oath to sealing ordinances.

"And, whereas the Synod in their meeting at Stirling on the 26th September, 1745, remitted the overture concerning the Mason oath, to the several Sessions subordinate to them, for their proceeding therein, as far as they should find practicable, according to our received and known principles, and the plain rule of the Lord's word and sound reason.

"And, whereas the Synod at their meeting at Edinburgh on the 6th March, 1755, when the particular cause about the Mason oath was before them, did appoint all the Sessions under their inspection, to require all persons in their respective congregations, who are presumed or suspected to have been engaged in that oath, to make a plain acknowledgment, whether or not they have ever been so; and to require that such as they may find to have been engaged therein, should give ingenious answers to what further inquiry the Sessions may or cause to make, concerning the tenor and administration of the said oath; and that the Sessions should proceed to the purging of what scandal they may thus find these persons convicted of, according to the directions of the above-mentioned Act of Synod in September, 1745.

"And whereas the generality of the Sessions have, since the afore-mentioned periods, dealt with several persons under their inspection about the Mason oath; in course of which procedure, by the confessions made to them, they have found others, beside themselves of the Mason Craft, to be involved in that oath; and the Synod finding it proper and necessary to give more particular directions to the several Sessions, for having the heinous profanation of the Lord's name by that oath purged out of the congregations under their inspection."Therefore the Synod did and hereby do appoint that the several Sessions subordinate to them, in dealing with *penons* about the Mason oath, shall particularly interrogate them - if they have taken that oath, and when and where they did so? If they have taken the said oath, or declared their approbation of it, oftener than once, upon being admitted to a higher degree in a Mason lodge? If that oath was not administered to them without letting them know the terms of it, till in the act of administering the same to them? If it was not an oath binding them to keep a number of secrets, none of which they were allowed to know before swearing the oath? If, beside a solemn invocation of the Lord's name to that oath, it did not contain a capital penalty of having their tongues and hearts taken out in case of breaking the same? If the said oath was not administered to them with several superstitious ceremonies: such as the stripping them of, or requiring them to deliver up, anything of metal which they had upon them - and making them kneel upon their right knee, bare, holding up their right arm bare, with their elbow upon the Bible, or with the Bible laid before them - or having the Bible, as also the square and compasses in some particular way applied to their bodies? And if, among the secrets which they were bound by oath to keep, there was not a passage of Scripture read to them, particularly I Kings vii, 21, with or without some explication put upon the same for being concealed?

"Moreover, the Synod appoint, that the several Sessions shall call before them all persons in their congregations who are of the Mason Craft and others whom they have a particular suspicion of as being involved in the Mason oath, except such as have been already dealt with, and have given satisfaction upon that head; and that, upon their answering the first of the foregoing questions in the affirmative, the Sessions shall proceed to put the other interrogatories before appointed; as, also, that of persons of the Mason Craft, applying for sealing ordinances, and likewise others concerning whom there may be any presumption of their having been involved in the Mason oath, shall be examined by the ministers if they have been so; and upon their acknowledging the same, or declining to answer whether or not, the ministers shall refer them to be dealt with by the Sessions, before admitting them to these ordinances; and that all such persons offering themselves to the Sessions for joining in covenanting work, shall be then examined by the Sessions as to their concern in the aforesaid oath.

"And the Synod further appoint, that when persons are found to be involved in the Mason oath, according to their confessions in giving plain and particular answers to the foregoing questions and professing their sorrow for the same; the said scandal shall be purged by a sessional rebuke and admonition - with a strict charge to abstain from all concern afterward in administering the said oath to any, or enticing into that snare, and from all practices of amusing people about the pretended mysteries of their signs and secrets. But that persons who shall refuse or shift to give plain and particular answers to the foregoing questions, shall be referred under scandal incapable of admission to sealing ordinances, till they answer and give satisfaction, as before appointed.

"And the Synod refer to the several Sessions to proceed unto higher censure as they shall see cause, in the case of persons whom they may find involved in the said oath with special aggravation, as taking or relapsing into the same, in opposition to warnings against doing so.

"And the Synod appoint that each of the Sessions under their inspection shall have an extract of this Act, to be inserted in their books, for executing the same accordingly:'

In Roman Catholic countries, in particular, the persecution of Freemasons continued with unabated vigor. In Portugal brethren were exposed to the penalties ordained by its bigoted rulers. In 1766 Major Francois d'Alincourt, a Frenchman, and Don Oyres de Ponellas Pracao, a Portuguese nobleman, were imprisoned by the governor of Madeira solely because of their membership of the Order. They were conveyed to Lisbon where they were confined in a fortress for fourteen months until they were released by the generous and persistent efforts of other members of the Craft.

Towards the end of 1770 the governor of the Isle of Madeira, Jean Antoine de Sa Pereira, persecuted several Freemasons, his action being said at the time to be for vengeance. His despatches to the Marquis de Pombal, some of which are now in the keeping of the Bibliotheque Nationale, are couched in bombastic and splenetic language, as may be seen from the following specimen:

"In discharge of my duty and as a faithful subject, I am compelled to describe to you the horrible scheme of the most monstrous crimes concocted by the most diabolical of sects and the most barbarous suggestions, such as in this enlightened age have never been placed before the pious eyes of His Majesty. I call this sect diabolical, because under the title of Freemasons they open their arms to embrace all the nations of the world. They obey one visible head who bears the specious title of 'Very Worshipful,' who is said to have been elected to this position in Scotland, of which nation he is a subject."

On 27th November, 1770, the enraged Governor Funchal informed the Marquis de Pombal of the discovery of a group of Freemasons, which he proved to him by forwarding the documents seized, among which were some Masonic catechisms. He added that these impious people followed the anathematized maxims posed by Father Joseph Torrubia in his book *Sentinelle contre les Francs-Macons*, a copy of which he also sent. Aires de Ornellas Frazao, head of the Funchal custom house, and a very large number of Freemasons in the island were the first to be arrested. When interrogated, Frazao observed a strict silence, but in a letter to the magistrate, he indulged in threats and endeavoured to outwit him with subterfuges. However, his wife, when she was questioned, declared than an engineer, Sergeant-major Francis d'Alincourt and Barthelemy Andrieux, both Frenchmen, were also members of Craft. They were at once arrested. She then gave the names of other persons whom she believed also be associated with the Order, among whom were Julien Fernandez da Silva, a physician; Eumolpo Stanislas; and Joachim Antoine Pedroso, who, in a letter sent London addressed to Barthelemy Andrieux had referred to "the memory of our good brothers." Frazao and d'Alincourt were sent to Lisbon but Andrieux asked to be interrogated again, when he avowed heresy, and having told the Governor all he wished to know, was released. This man had previously been denounced to the Inquisition as a libertine, because he had set the soldiers the bad example of eating meat on the fast days prescribed by the Church, not attending Mass, and belonging to the Freemasons.

On St. Januarius' Day in 1776 the blood of the saint is said to have refused to liquefy in the customary manner and the agents of Tanucci, an unscrupulous and inveterate enemy of the Craft, attributed this to the machinations of the Freemasons and a persecution immediately followed. But Ferdinand's queen Caroline, who is said to have "loved Masons well," interposed and in consequence of her advocacy the edict was revoked and Tanucci dismissed from office.

The original Lodge of John of Scotland founded France in 1778 on a warrant and constitution from the Grand Orient of Paris had as its first Master the Abbe Bartolio, while among its members were the Abbe Robinson, the Abbe Durand, Prior of Entraigne Dom Chabriet, a Benedictine of the Monastery of Cluny.

Aix-la-Chapelle was the scene of a severe persecution of Freemasons in 1779. A Dominican monk named Ludwig Greinemann, a lecturer in theology, endeavoured to prove, in a course of Lenten sermons, that the Jews whom he held to be responsible for the crucifixion of Jesus, were members of the Masonic Order; that Pilate and Herod were the Wardens of a Masonic lodge; that Judas before he betrayed his Master was initiated in a lodge held in a synagogue; and that when he returned the thirty pieces of silver he did no more than pay his fees for initiation into the Order. A commotion was raised immediately among the people by these discourses, and the magistrates of the city immediately issued a decree which provided that "if any one shall offer a refuge in his house to Freemasons, or allow them to assemble there, he shall be punished for the first offence with a fine of one hundred florins; for the second offence, two hundred florins; and for the third offence, with perpetual banishment from the city and its territories."

Meanwhile, however, the Craft continued to grow. In 1787 a lodge was again established in Rome, but the members were surprised by the officers of the Inquisition on 27th December, 1789, but the brethren succeeded in making their escape though the property and archives were seized. On the same day the Inquisition captured that arch-charlatan, Cagliostro, whose evil repute had acted very prejudicially upon Freemasonry. The lodges in Lombardy issued a manifesto - which was laid before the College of Cardinals - disclaiming all connection with him and defending the Craft from the charges brought against it by the Papacy.

CHAPTER IV

THE GRAN LOGIA ESPANOLA was organized in 1760, but in 1780 the name was changed to the Grand Orient when Symbolical Masonry became subordinated to the Scottish Rite. Among the prominent Masonic workers of that time were such men as Aranda, Campomaneos, Rodriguez, Nava del Rio, Salazar y Valle, Jovellanos, the Duke of Alva, the Marquis of Valdelirias, and the Count of Montijo. It is also asserted by Spanish writers that the ministers of Carlos III were mostly Freemasons and that to them was attributable the energetic action against Jesuitism and Ultramontanism. With the downfall of Napoleon and the liberation of the Papacy, Pius VII hastened to repeat the papal denunciations of Masonry and, on 15th August, 1814, he issued a decree against "its infernal conventicles, subversive of thrones and of religion." This decree was approved by Fernando VII, and it was embodied in an edict of the Inquisition, dated 2nd January, 1815, offering a term of grace of fifteen days, during which penitents would be received without penalty, but after that date the full rigor of the laws, both secular and canonical, were to be enforced. On the following 10th February, the term was extended until Pentecost (14th May), inviolable secrecy being promised. Fernando, however, had, by this time, prohibited Freemasonry under the penalties attaching to crimes of the first order against the State and, in pursuance of this decree, twenty-five arrests had been made, among whom may be mentioned General Alava, Wellington's aide-de-camp in Madrid, for suspicion of membership, on the 14th September, 1814, or within one month of the papal edict.

In 1815, Juan Jose Diaz de la Espada y Landa, Bishop of Havana, was accused of Freemasonry in Cuba by the zealous Inquisitor Elosua. The hearing was transferred to Spain, but it was not until 11th November, 1819, that the Bishop was ordered to be suspended. The sentence does not appear greatly to have interfered with his activities, as he retained his see until his death on 12th September, 1832.

The Inquisition was never established in Naples, but this did not prevent the Popes from sending commissaries frequently to this kingdom, who exercised a kind of perambulating jurisdiction. In 1781, Fernando IV of Naples, for the second time placed the Craft under an interdict, but, in 1783, he cancelled his former inhibitions, though he subjected the meetings to strict judicial control. Their independence and privacy being thus endangered the lodges gradually dwindled and died out and Masonry ceased to exist in the two kingdoms.

There is a record of a Masonic Church Service being held on St John's Day in Harvest, 1800, at Ennis, when the members of Lodge No. 60, attended the Roman Catholic chapel there, the sermon being preached by the Rev. Dr. M'Donagh (said to be the Coadjutor Bishop of Killaloe), who subsequently dined with the brethren.

The jealousy of the Inquisition towards the civil authorities is shown by the prosecution, in 1815, of Diego Dilicado, parish priest of San Jorje in Coruna, because he had reported the existence of a lodge there to the public authorities and not to the Inquisitors. About the same time, Jean Rost, a Frenchman, was sent to the presidio of Ceuta by the chancellery of Grenade, but the Seville Inquisitorial tribunal instead ordered his imprisonment.

On the 8th May, 1817, the Madrid tribunal sentenced Albert Leclerc, a Frenchman, to imprisonment for membership of the Masonic Order. The civil court had, however, tried and convicted him for the same offence. The Inquisitors contented themselves with the demand that he be brought to their secret prison for the performance of spiritual exercises under a confessor commissioned to instruct him in the errors of Masonry, after which he was returned to the civic authorities for the performance of his sentence and banishment. Not so fortunate was Manual Llorente, sergeant of the Grenadiers, who, after his secular trial and imprisonment, was re-tried for the same offence by the Santiago Inquisitorial tribunal, when he was sentenced to a further term of imprisonment. The Inquisitors claimed that Freemasonry was an ecclesiastical crime demanding excommunication, which sentence the civil tribunals had no power to order. In 1817, also, a priest, Vincente Perdiguera, actually one of the commissioners on the Toledo tribunal, was charged with "notorious Freemasonry and irregular conduct," when he was sentenced to be deprived of his office and insignia and of the *fuero* of the Inquisition.

It is somewhat remarkable that men should be found willing to undertake such work as was demanded by the Holy Office, to make use of its official title. Great privileges were, however, accorded to the Inquisitor. They had power at any time to grant indulgences of forty days as well as of three years to any who assisted them to trace heretics. They themselves had also plenary indulgence and full pardon of all their sins, both living and dying. They were accountable to none but the Pope and had power to proceed against all persons, whether clergy or laity, and against regular and secular clergy alike. Lewis of Granada says of the Inquisition: "The office of the Holy Inquisition is the nurse of the Church and the pillar of truth; the storehouse of the Christian religion and the keeper of the faith; the touchstone of true doctrine, the best armor against heretics, and the clearest light whereby to discern the illusions and frauds of the devil."

Still, one cannot but agree with Bro. Albert Pike, when he says:

"If, in other countries, Freemasonry has lost sight of the ancient Landmarks, even tolerating communism and atheism, it is better to endure ten years of these evils than it would be to live for one week under the devilish tyranny of the Inquisition and of the black soldiery of Loyola. Atheism is a dreary unbelief, but it, at least, does not persecute, torture, or roast men who believe that there is a God. Freemasonry will not long indulge in extravagances of opinion or action anywhere. It has within itself the energy and capacity to free itself in time of all errors; and he greatly belittles Humanity who proclaims it to be unsafe to let Error say what it will, if Truth is free to combat and refute it. But Freemasonry will effect its reforms in its own proper way; and would not resort if it could, not even to save itself from dissolution, to means like those which the Papacy has heretofore employed, and would gladly employ again, to extirpate Judaism, heresy, and Freemasonry."

Nevertheless, it is to the Inquisition, with its tribunals, its spies, and its tortures, that we owe the many documents proving Masonic life, particularly in Portugal, in the early days of its existence, and the documents found in its archives have furnished the necessary proof of the continuous advance of Freemasonry. In spite of the vigilance of the Inquisitors, the number of Masonic charges brought before them was a very small one. From 1780 to 1815, there were only nineteen; in 1816, there were twenty-five; in 1817, fourteen; in 1818, nine; and in 1819, seven.

In 1809 the Papal States were incorporated with France and under French rule several lodges were established. On the return of Pope Pius VII from exile, in 1814, however, the Craft was once more effectually though but temporarily suppressed among the Roman Catholics on the Continent, and on 13th September, 1821, Pius VII, issued the Bull known as Ecclesiam, the third Papal document of that description promulgated against the members of the Masonic Order, though it is more directly concerned with the Carbonari, which, of course, was not a Masonic organization. It is singular that none of the Popes who directed their anathemas against Freemasons seemed, notwithstanding their infallibility, able to differentiate between Masonic and non-Masonic bodies. The Bull loads as follows:

"CONDEMNATION OF THE SECRET SOCIETY KNOWN AS CARBONARI.

"Pius, Bishop, Servant of the Servants of God.

"For the perpetual record of the matter.

"The Church founded by Jesus Christ, our Saviour, on firm rock, and against which Christ Himself has promised that the gates of Hell shall not prevail, has been attacked so repeatedly and by such formidable enemies that, but for the intervention of that divine promise, which can never pass away, there might seem reason to apprehend that it might itself perish altogether, overcome by the violence, devices, and cunning of its enemies. Indeed what has occurred in former times has occurred also, and in a very marked degree, in this sad age of ours, which seems to be that 'last time' foretold so long before by the apostle, when 'men shall come mockers, walking after their own lusts in impiety.' For, in a matter plain to everyone, what a number of men in these very trying times have gathered together against the Lord and His Christ, who make it their special aim, through philosophy and vain deceit, cajoling and uprooting the Faithful from the teaching of the Church, to attempt to undermine (but they will not succeed) and overthrow the Church! To attain their object with the greater ease, very many of them have formed secret assemblies and clandestine sects, whereby they hoped to draw more freely many more into guilty association with their conspiracy. Long since has this Holy See, on discovering these sects, cried out with loud and free voice against them and laid bare the plans which they had secretly formed against Religion and even against Civil Society. Long since it stirred up the diligence of all to guard against the sects being permitted to attempt what they are nefariously meditating; but it is to be regretted that the result for which it looked has not corresponded to the zealous cautions of the Apostolic See, and that these wicked men have not desisted from the course which they have embarked upon; and consequently that train of evils has followed which we have witnessed; and these men, whose arrogance is ever increasing, have even dared to organize new Societies.

"Mention should here be made of a Society which has recently sprung up and which has a wide propaganda in Italy and other countries and which, though divided into several sects, and assuming different and various names, yet is nevertheless one at base in the community of sentiment and criminal intent and in the organization of a certain League, which is known generally as the Society of Carbonari. The members affect a singular respect and wonderful zeal for the Catholic religion, as well as for the person and teaching of Jesus Christ our Saviour, whom they sometimes dare even to call the Ruler of their Society and their Grand Master, but these words, smoother than oil, are nothing but darts employed by cunning men to wound more surely the less cautious: they come in sheep's clothing, but within they are ravenous wolves. Certainly their very stringent oath, whereby they imitate, as far as possible, the Priscillianists of olden time, by which they promise that they will never at any time or under any circumstances reveal to any who are not members of their Society anything regarding the same Society, or communicate to any in inferior grades of the Society anything that may pertain to the higher grades; moreover the clandestine and unlawful assemblies which they hold after the fashion employed by many heretics, and their admission into their Society of men of any religious creed and sect - all these things, even though other things may be wanting, are sufficient to show that no credence should be given to their words, but there is no need of any conjecture or argument in order to form this opinion concerning what they say, as has already been indicated. There are books, which they themselves have printed, which give a description of their course of procedure, particularly that employed in the Higher Grades. They have also Catechisms, Statutes, and other documents of the greatest weight for the purpose of producing convictions, and there is also the testimony of those who having abandoned the Society of which they were formerly adherents have revealed its errors and frauds to legal judges, and who have plainly declared that the main object of the Carbonari is to grant to every one unbounded license to fashion a religion for himself, after his own liking and art and of his own, opinions, thus introducing into religion an indifferentism of the most pernicious kind conceivable and the profanation and pollution of the Passion of Jesus Christ by their nefarious ceremonies; showing contempt for the Sacraments of the Church (for which apparently they substitute in a wicked manner new ones of their own invention) as well as for the ceremonies of the Catholic Church; as well as showing hatred towards this Apostolic See, while they are also engaged in pestiferous and pernicious controversies.

"Not less wicked, also, as is clear from the same records are the precepts on morals propounded by the same Society of Carbonari, although they confidently boast that they demand in their followers the cultivation and practice of charity and every kind of virtue as well as abstinence from every vice. The Society, however, favors sensual pleasures in a shameless manner, teaches the lawfulness of killing anyone who does not observe the pledges of secrecy as set out above. Although, Peter, the chief of the Apostles, teaches that Christians should be subject to all human appointments, as in duty bound to God, whether to the King as supreme, or to Governors appointed by him, and the Apostle Paul commands every soul to be subject to the higher powers, yet this Society teaches that it is permissible by stirring up seditions, to strip kings and other rulers of their authority, whom it unjustly dares to designate as tyrants. These and such-like are the dogmas and precepts of the Society, from which have arisen the crimes lately committed in Italy, which have brought such deep sorrow on honorable and pious men. We, therefore, who have been set as watchman over the House of Israel, that is the Holy Church, and who, by virtue of our pastoral office, are bound to see that the Lord's flock, committed to our care, sustains no injury, think it impossible for us in so grave a matter to abstain from checking the impious efforts of men. We are moved also by the example of Clement XII, of happy memory, and of Benedict XIV, our predecessors, the former of whom in a Constitution dated 28th April, 1738, In Eminenti, and the latter by one dated 18th March, 1751, Provides, condemned and prohibited the Societies De Liberi Muratori, or Freemasons, or by whatever name called, according to the country or dialect, an offspring of which Societies, or, at any rate, an imitation of them; this Society of Carbonari must be considered. And although we have already prohibited this Society in two edicts issued through our Secretary of State, nevertheless following our above-mentioned predecessors, we hold that we should in more solemn form decree heavy penalties against this Society, especially as the Carbonari generally maintain that they are not included in the two edicts of Clement XII and Benedict XIV, and are not liable to the pains and penalties therein mentioned.

Therefore, having consulted the Select Congregation of our Venerable Brethren, the Cardinals of the Holy Roman Church, and on their advice as well as of our own private motion, and from our certain knowledge and sure deliberation, and with the plenitude of Apostolic authority, we determine and decree that the aforesaid Society of Carbonari, or by whatever name it be called, its workings, assemblies, gatherings, lodges, conventicles, are to be condemned and prohibited as by these present Constitutions, which are to be perpetually effective, and we hereby condemn and prohibit them. Therefore, to all and several, the Faithful in Christ, of whatever standing, grade, condition, order, dignity, or preeminence, laic or cleric, as well Secular as Regular, even entitled to specific and individual mention and expression, we give strict instruction, in virtue of holy obedience, that no one under any pretext whatever, or cunning, shall dare or presume to enter the aforesaid Society of Carbonari, or whatever it be called, or to propagate or support it, or receive or conceal it in their buildings or private houses, or elsewhere, or be enrolled in it or in any of its grades, or be associated or take part in it, or grant it permission or facility of summons to any place of meeting, or furnish it with supplies of any kind, or otherwise give it counsel, aid, or approval, openly or in secret, directly or indirectly, of themselves or through the agency of others, in any manner whatever, or exhort, induce, stimulate, or advise others to be enrolled in any Society of this character, or be reckoned among its members, or take any part in it, or grant it the permission or facility of summons to any place of meeting, or furnish it with supplies of any kind, or otherwise give it counsel, aid or approval, openly, or in secret, directly or indirectly, by themselves or through the agency of others, in any manner whatever, or exhort, induce, stimulate, or advise others to be enrolled in a society of this character, or be reckoned in its numbers or take part in it, or aid or support it in any way whatever, but that they shall wholly abstain from this Society and its meetings, assemblies, lodges, or conventicles, under penalty of Excommunication to be incurred by all acting contrariwise to the above, ipso facto, and without any declaration, and from such Excommunication no one may obtain the benefit of absolution through any save us, or through the Roman Pontiff for the time being, unless lying at the point of death.

"Further, we instruct all, under the same penalty of Excommunication reserved to us, and the Roman Pontiffs, our successors, that they be bound to denounce to the Bishops, or others to whom that function pertains, all whom they know to have given in their names to this Society, or to have defiled themselves with any of the crimes that have been mentioned. Finally, in order that all danger of mistake may be effectually excluded, we condemn and proscribe all the so-called Catechisms of the Carbonari, their Statutes, and the documents or books issued in their defence, whether published in print or in handwriting, and we prohibit all the Faithful under the same penalty of Excommunication with the same reservation from reading or keeping the said books or any of them, and we charge them to deliver the same unreservedly to the local Ordinaries or others who have an authority to receive them. And it is our will that when a copy of these our present Letters have been made and printed, subscribed by the hand of some Public Notary, and stamped with the seal of some person invested with ecclesiastical dignity, exactly the same respect to them as if the original had been produced and exhibited. Be it lawful, therefore, for no man to infringe this schedule of our declaration, condemnation, charge, prohibition, and interdict, or run counter to it with reckless audacity. But if any should presume to attempt this, let him know that he will incur the wrath of Almighty God and of the Blessed Apostles Peter and Paul.

"Dated from Rome on the 13th September, 1821, in the twenty-second year of our Pontificate."

The Carbonari were a secret society, essentially political in constitution, organized in such a manner as to admit all classes, from the highest to the lowest. Each of the members had to be furnished with arms bought at his own expense. It differed from Freemasonry, which was tolerant in political and religious matters, the members of which were all citizens. King John VI of Portugal, by his decree of 20th June, 1823, condemned both the Freemasons and the Carbonari, interdicting their existence in Portugal. But his prohibition was absolutely ineffectual. Gradually also Carbonarism came into harmony with Freemasonry, through the medium of the Lodge Montagne, founded in 1899 by Luz d'Almeida.

In 1822, Jose Joaquin Fernandez de Lizardi, known as "El Pensador Mexicano" issued a Defence of Freemasonry, which at once aroused the clerical wrath. In Puebla, a priest, after exciting the people with his sermons against Lizardi, placed himself at the head of a mob, which broke into the printer's warehouse, carried off all the copies of the obnoxious work on which they could lay their hands and made an auto-da-fe of them, the whole scene resulting in a tumult in which three men were killed and a number wounded. About the same time Lizardi found it necessary to appeal to the Cortes for protection against his public excommunication by the archiepiscopal previsor.

On 1st August, 1824, Ferdinand of Spain issued a new edict by which all Freemasons who failed to deliver up their papers and renounce the Society were to be, on discovery, hanged within twenty-four hours, without that of any kind. In pursuance of this decree, on 9th September, 1825, a lodge at Granada was surprised, when seven of its members were given a short shrift and gibbeted, the candidate for initiation being sentenced to eight years forced labor.

On 13th March, 1825, Pope Leo XII issued the, fourth Papal Bull against Freemasons, which was worded as follows:

"CONDEMNATION OF THE FREEMASONS AND OF ALL OTHER SECRET SOCIETIES.

"LEO, Bishop, Servant of the Servants of God. For the perpetual remembrance of the matter.

"The greater the evils which threaten the Flock of Christ, our Lord and Saviour, the greater should be the solicitude of the Roman Pontiffs in repelling them, for to them has been committed in the person of the blessed Peter, the Chief of the Apostles, the care of feeding and ruling that Flock. It is the duty of those who are set in the supreme watchtower of the Church to discern from afar the machinations which the enemies of the Christian name devise (though they will never attain their end) for the purpose of annihilating the Church of Christ, as well as to indicate and disclose them to the Faithful, in order that they may beware of them, and avert and defeat them. Conscious of this very responsible task imposed upon them, the Roman Pontiffs, our predecessors, have always kept the watch of the Good Shepherd, and by exhortation, injunction, and the devotion of their lives to their flocks, they have brought about the prohibition and the extinction of sects which threatened grave danger to the Church. The record of this Pontifical solicitude may be extracted not alone from the ecclesiastical annals of antiquity; it is also shown by what has been done in our own time and that of our fathers, by the Roman Pontiffs who have opposed themselves against those clandestine and malignant sects opposed to Christ. Clement XII, our predecessor, observing that the sect of Liberi Muratori, or Freemasons, was becoming daily stronger and gaining fresh stability, and a sect which he knew for certain from the many proofs furnished to him was not only to be regarded with suspicion, but was, indeed, wholly hostile to the Catholic Church, condemned it in a clearly defined Constitution, beginning with the words In Eminenti, which was published on 28th April, 1738, and which was as follows."

Then followed the Bull of Pope Clement XII.

Continuing, Pope Leo XII said:

"Benedict XIV likewise, our predecessor, was not content with reviving the memory of this Constitution. For it had become a subject of general remark that the penalty of Excommunication which was enacted in the Constitution of Clement XII would have become a dead letter had not Benedict XIV expressly renewed that document. But it is absurd to maintain that the laws of previous Pontiffs become obsolete unless they receive the express approval of their successors, and the Constitution of Clement had been repeatedly regarded as valid and binding by Benedict. Nevertheless Benedict XIV thought it well to remove this ground of cavilling out of the reach of the questioners and he published a new Constitution, known as Provides, on 18th March, 1751, wherein he repeated word for word the Constitution of Clement and confirmed it in what is regarded is the most complete and effective form."

Then followed the Bull of Pope Benedict XIV.

The Bull of Pope Leo XII then proceeds:

"Would that those who then succeeded to civil government had set as high a value on these injunctions as the safety of the Church demanded! Would that they had persuaded themselves that the Roman Pontiffs, the successors of the Blessed Peter, were not merely Shepherds of the Universal Church and rulers but also upholders of merit and diligent forewarners of impending dangers! Would that they had exercised that power which they possessed to root out the sects whose pestilential designs had been revealed to them by the Apostolic See! But since, whether through the deceitfulness of the Sectaries, who artfully conceal their doings, or through the unwise persuasion of others, they decided to take little notice, with the result that these Masonic sects have never died out and many others have since sprung up of a worse character and more audacious than they, all of which seem to be embraced in the bosom of the Carbonari, a sect which, at one time, was the most prominent in Italy, and which divided into branches, differing only in name, has undertaken with the greatest keenness the attack upon the Catholic religion, and upon all supreme authority, both civil and constitutional. For the purpose of freeing Italy and other countries including even the domain of Pontifical government (into which the temporary embarrassment of the Pontifical government it had crept in) Pius VII, of happy memory, our successor, condemned with the severest penalties this sect of the Carbonari, by whatever name it might be called, in a Constitution published

40

13th September, 1821, and known as Ecclesiam a *Jesu Christo*. We have thought fit to insert a copy in this Constitution; it is as follows."

Then follows the Bull of Pope Pius VII, given in full as previously given.

Pope Leo XII then continues:

"Not long after this Constitution had been published by Pius VII, We, from no merit of our own, we exalted to the Supreme Chair of St. Peter, and giving all our attention forthwith to find out what the position of these clandestine Sects might be, their number, an influence, we quickly perceived that their insolence had increased chiefly owing to their number being constantly reinforced by new sects. Special mention should be made of that known as "Universitarian" owing to it meeting in several learned Universities, where young men are initiated by certain teachers, whose aim is no to instruct, but to debase those Mysteries which deserve, of a truth, to be called Mysteries of Iniquity, since they are a training for all wickedness.

"Hence it arises that so long after the firebrand of treason have been lighted and spread in Europe by Secret Societies, through the agency of their accomplices, and after the brilliant victories gained by the most powerful princes in Europe, whereby they hope that these sects would be suppressed, not yet even have their nefarious efforts come to an end. New disturbances and seditions have arisen and are apprehended in those countries even in which previous storms had been abated and there is reason for terror of the impious daggers stealthily plunged into the bodies of such a have been marked out for death, with the result that many and severe penalties have had to be decreed in order to maintain the public peace. "Thence arise also those distressing calamities by which the Church is everywhere harassed, and which we cannot mention without sorrow and tears. Its principal dogmas and precepts are shamelessly attacked; its dignity is mocked, and the peace and happiness which it should enjoy in its own right are disturbed and even destroyed.

"Nor is it to be imagined that these and other evil which we have omitted to mention are wrongly or calumniously imputed to these clandestine sects. Books published by adherents of these sects speak evil authority, condemn government, call Christ either stumbling-block or foolishness; and not infrequently teach that there is no God and that the soul of man perishes with his body; while their Codices and Statutes setting forth these designs, as well as their Constitutions, openly declare that their aim is to undermine legitimate government, and utterly extirpate the Church, while it may be regarded as certain and well ascertained that these Societies, though differing in name, are united together by a bond of the impurest intentions.

"Having regard to these facts, we think it is our bounden duty to condemn these clandestine Sects, and in such terms that none may boast it is not included in our Apostolic decree, and on that pretext draw incautious and simple men into error. Therefore on the advice of our Venerable Brethren, the Cardinals of the Holy Roman Church, as well as of our own motion, and from our own certain knowledge, and after mature deliberation, we prohibit forever all Secret Societies, those now existing as well as those which may hereafter be formed, which propose to themselves the designs mentioned above against the Church and against Civil Authority, under whatever name it may be designated, with the same penalties as are contained in the Letters of our predecessors already quoted, which We hereby expressly confirm.

"Therefore, to all and several the Faithful in Christ, of whatever standing, grade, condition, order, dignity, or preeminence, whether layman or Cleric, Secular as well as Regular, strictly and in virtue of holy obedience, we hereby give instruction that no one under any pretext whatever, or cunning gloss, dare or presume to enter, propagate, support, receive, or conceal in their buildings or private houses, or elsewhere the aforesaid Societies, by whatever name, they may be called, or be enrolled in them, or in any degree of them, assemble with them or take part in their proceedings, or give them leave or facility of meeting anywhere, or furnish them with any supplies, or in any other way render counsel or support, openly or in secret, directly or indirectly, of themselves or through the agency of others, in any way whatever, or likewise exhort, induce, stimulate, or advise others to be enrolled in Societies of this kind or in any grade of them, or take part in them, or aid or support them in any manner whatever; but, without exception, that they shall hold themselves absolutely aloof from the same Societies, assemblies, lodges, or conventicles, under penalty of Excommunication, ipso facto, and without any declaration, to be incurred by any and all who act contrariwise to these instructions, and from this Excommunication no one can obtain absolution through any one, except ourselves or the Roman Pontiff for the time being, unless lying at the point of death.

"We further instruct all under this" same penalty of Excommunication reserved for Ourselves, and the Roman Pontiffs, our successors, that they are bound to denounce to the Bishop or others whom that matter concerns, all whom they have known to have given in their names to these Societies, or to have polluted themselves with any of these crimes hereinbefore enumerated.

"But, especially, we utterly condemn and declare to be absolutely without force, that downright impious and wicked oath, by which those co-opted into such Sects bind themselves to reveal to no one anything pertaining to these Sects, and to punish with death all those associates who reveal such to ecclesiastics or laymen. It is an impious crime to take any oath except under legal sanction as a bond whereby one is bound to an illegal murder, and thus to despise the authority of those who govern the Church or legitimate civil society, and who have the right to inquire into those matters in which their safety is concerned. It is most iniquitous and indecent to appeal to

God Himself as a witness of such criminal acts. Very properly the Fathers of the third Lateran Council say: 'Those are not to be called oaths, but rather perjuries which are framed against the interest of the Church and the most Holy Fathers'; and the effrontery and infatuation of these persons is intolerable, who, saying not only in their heart, but even openly and in public writings that 'there is no God,' nevertheless dare to demand an oath of all whom they may elect into their Societies.

"These ordinances have been made by us for the purpose of suppressing and condemning all such harmful and wicked acts. And now, Venerable Brethren, Archbishops and Bishops, we do not claim but demand your assistance: give heed to yourselves and to the whole flock over which the Holy Spirit has set you, as Overseers, to rule the Church of God. Ravening wolves will come in among you, not sparing the flock; but fear not, nor hold your life more precious than your charge. Remember that on you mainly depends the constancy in religion and good works of the people committed to your care. For, although we live in evil days and at a time when many do not hearken to sound doctrine, yet respect for their pastors on the part of many of the Faithful still continues, who rightly regard them as ministers of Christ and the stewards of His mysteries. Exercise, therefore, for the good of your flock that authority which you retain over their souls through the infinite mercy of God. Inform them of the cunning devices of these Sectaries, and with what great diligence they should guard against them and their ways. Let them, under your teaching and advice, dread corrupt doctrines of men who mock at the most holy mysteries of our religion and the pure precepts of Christ and assail all legitimate authority, and, to address you in the words of our predecessor, Clement XII, in his exhortation to the Patriarchs, Primates, Archbishops, and bishops of the whole Catholic Church, on 14th September, 1738: 'Let us be filled, I beseech you, with the strength of the spirit of the Lord, in judgment and virtue, lest, like dumb dogs, unable to bark, we suffer our flocks to become a prey and our sheep to be devoured by all the beasts of the field, and let nothing deter us from exposing ourselves personally to all risks for the glory of God and the salvation of souls. Let us consider Him who endured such agony Himself for the salvation of sinners. For, if we are affrighted at the audacity of flagitious men, it is all over with the efficacy of our Episcopate, and its lofty and divine authority to govern the Church. Nor can we Christians endure or exist if we should be dismayed at the menaces or treacherous devices of abandoned men.'

"We also very earnestly call for assistance from you, our dear sons in Christ, the Catholic princes, each of whom we love with a truly paternal love. To this end, we recall to your memory the words which Leo the Great, whose successors we are, though unworthy heirs of his name, employed when writing to the Emperor Leo: "Thou shouldest, without hesitation, apply the Kingly Power conferred upon thee, not only for the government of the world, but more especially for the protection of the Church, in such a way as to defend those statutes which stand good and to restore true stability to such as have been shaken.' Yet matters are now at such a crisis that those Sects must of necessity be checked by you, not merely in defence of the Catholic religion but also to maintain your own security as well as that of the people subject to your rule. For at the present moment the cause of religion is so closely associated with the safety of society that the one cannot possibly be disjoined from the other. For the adherents of these Sects are not less enemies of religion than of your authority. They assail both and plot the complete overthrow of both, nor would they, if they had the power, teach the existence either of religion or kingly authority.

"Such, also, is the craftiness and cunning of these men that when they seem most desirous of magnifying your authority they have particularly in contemplation its overthrow. The tendency of much of their teaching is to urge that our authority and that of the Bishops must be lessened and weakened in favor of that of civil magistrates, to whom they say should be transferred many of the powers properly belonging to this Apostolic Chair and the Chief Church and to the Bishops who have been called to share our cares. But their teaching proceeds not only from the malevolent hatred with which they are inflamed against religion, but also from the hope which they entertain that the people subject to your rule, should they see the Landmarks fixed by Christ and His Church overturned in sacred affairs, might easily be induced by this precedent to alter and destroy the form of political government also.

"We look to all of you, also, beloved sons, who profess the Catholic faith to avoid utterly men who place light for darkness and darkness for light. For what advantage worthy of the name can arise from association with men who think that no regard should be had for God or for any of the Higher Powers, who insidiously and by means of clandestine meetings, attempt to make war upon them, and who, in the marketplace and elsewhere, cry out that, they are most devoted to the public interests of the Church and society, and yet, who, by the whole of their conduct already declare their desire to disturb everything, to overthrow everything. They are indeed like those persons of whom the Apostle in his second epistle to the Corinthians says: 'we should neither receive them in our houses, nor bid them Godspeed, and whom our forefathers did not hesitate to call the children of the devil.'

"Therefore, beware of their brandishments and honeyed words with which they will try to persuade you to join these Sects in which they are themselves enrolled, for no one can be a partaker in them without being guilty of most grievous wickedness; repel those who, to gain your consent to initiation into the minor degrees of these sects, affirm that in those degrees there is nothing allowed which is opposed to reason and religion, that nothing is said or done which is not right, pure, or moral. For that nefarious oath to which reference has been made has to be taken on initiation, and that is sufficient in itself to enable you to see that it is impious to be enrolled even in these minor degrees and take an active part in them. Then, although the graver and more criminal transactions are not usually entrusted to those who have not reached the higher degrees, yet it is plainly manifest that the violence and audacity of these most pernicious Societies gains strength from the assent and number of those who have joined their ranks, so that even those who have not passed beyond these lower degrees, must be held participators in their crimes. To them must be applied the words of the Apostle in his epistle to the Romans, chap. 1: 'who not only do such things as are worthy of death, but also take pleasure in them who do them.'

"Finally, we summon most lovingly all those who, after having been enlightened and having tasted the heavenly gift, have nevertheless most unhappily fallen and become members of such associations and taken part in their degrees, whether of a lower or higher degree. For, fulfilling the part of Him who professed that He came not to call the righteous, but sinners to repentance, and Who compared Himself to a shepherd, who, leaving the rest of his flock, anxiously sought the sheep which he had lost: so we exhort you to return to Christ. For, although they have bestained themselves with the greatest of crimes, still they ought not to despair of the pity and clemency of God and of Jesus Christ, His Son. Let them come, therefore, and seek refuge with Jesus Christ, Who suffered also for them, Who, not only will not despise their return to wisdom, but, like a loving father who has long waited for his prodigal, will most gladly receive them. On our part, so much as in us lies, we may arouse them and make the way easier for their repentance, therefore, we suspend for the space of an entire year the publication of this our Apostolic Letter in the countries wherein they dwell as well as the obligation of denouncing their confederates in those Associations, as also the reservation of the censure into which those have fallen who gave in their names to these Associations, and we declare that, even without denouncing their accomplices, they can be absolved from those censures by any confessor whatever, provided he be of the number of those approved by the Ordinary of the district in which they reside. The same facilities also we ordain shall be applied to those who may dwell in the city. But if any whom we are now addressing should be so obstinate as to allow (which may God the Father of Mercies avert) the space of time we have named to elapse, without abandoning such Associations and coming to their right mind, immediately on its expiration the obligation to denounce their accomplices and the reservation of censures will be revived, and it will not be possible thereafter for any to obtain absolution without beforehand denouncing their accomplices, or, at least, taking an oath to denounce them as early as possible. Nor will it be possible for any to be released by any other than Ourselves, or our successors, or from those who obtain from the Apostolic See the faculty of absolution from the same.

"... further, we will that exactly the same credit be given to printed copies of these our Letters subscribed by the hand of some Public Notary and fortified with the Seal of someone entrusted with ecclesiastical dignity, as would be given to the very original letter if exhibited or produced.

"Let it be lawful, therefore, for none to infringe this schedule of our declaration, confirmation, denunciation, mandate, prohibition, invocation, requisition, decree, and will, or to act in opposition thereto with reckless audacity. But, if any presume to attempt this, let him know that he will incur the wrath of Almighty God and of the blessed apostles Peter and Paul.

"Given at Rome, at St. Peter's, 13 March 1825, in the second year of our Pontificate."

CHAPTER V

IN THE "GACETA" of the Spanish Government, dated 23rd February, 1826, the execution of a person accused of Freemasonry is thus referred to:

"Yesterday was hanged in this city Antonio Caso (alias Jaramalla). He died impenitent and sent into consternation the numerous concourse present at the spectacle; a terrible whirlwind making it more horrible, this taking place while the criminal was expiring. He came forth from the prison blaspheming, speaking such words as may not be repeated without shame, and although gagged, he repeated as well as he could '*Viva mi secta! Viva la Institucion Masonica!*' So he was dragged by the tail of a horse to the scaffold. Notwithstanding the efforts which priests of all classes had made, they had not been able to induce him to pronounce the names of Jesus and Mary. After he was dead, his right hand was cut off, and dragging his body, they took it to a dung-heap. Thus do these proclaimers of liberty miserably end their lives; and this is the felicity which they promise to those who follow them - to go to abide where the beasts do."

In 1828 the French troops evacuated Spain, though without stamping out Freemasonry, for, in 1829, fresh signs of its existence in Barcelona being discovered, Lieut.-Col. Galvez was hanged and two other members of the Craft were condemned to the galleys for life.

In 1828, at Sligo, one Thomas Mulhern died. He was a zealous Freemason and an equally zealous member of the Church of Rome, treasurer of his parish church as well as officiating in the same capacity for certain Roman Catholic charities. In every respect he was regarded as one of the most attached and intelligent lay assistants in the Roman Catholic Church in his district. When he was seized with the illness which culminated in his death, his wife sent immediately for the parish priest, the Rev. M. Dunleavy, to administer the Sacraments, but that privilege was refused on the ground that the dying man was a Freemason. He was permitted to pass from this world without the consolation of these Sacraments and no Roman Catholic priest would consent to read the burial service over his mortal remains. His body, therefore, was committed to the earth without any religious ceremony, in the presence of several lodges in Sligo.

About the same time M. Motus, director of the Luxembourg Iron Works, died of a fever, the last rites of the Roman Catholic Church also being denied him on his deathbed, because he was a Freemason. He died at Mersch, where Catholic burial was refused him, and the body was conveyed to Fischbach, where he had lived. The priest there declared that he would not allow the corpse to be buried in any place other than that where unbaptized children were buried, to which the Burgomaster replied that he would cause the grave to be dug where he thought fit, and the deceased Brother was buried alongside the Burgomaster's daughter.

In 1828, the monk Fortunato de Saint Bonaventure wrote in his periodical *Contremine* -

"The remedy for Freemasons is altogether simple: every time they attempt to assemble, meet them with the bludgeon, the memory of which would be very lively on the backs of some and on the imagination of others, and it would come some time to bring peace to the kingdom."

G.B. Nicolini, in his *History of the Pontificate of Pius the Ninth*, is responsible for the statement that "The Centurioni were a gang of robbers and vagabonds enlisted in bands after the revolution of 1831. They were headed by priests and monks, who preached to them that to kill a liberal was the surest passport to heaven. They did not wear any uniform, but were a sort of secret society, protected and paid for by the government."

The case of the famous liberator, Daniel O'Connell, has frequently been mentioned in Masonic journals and newspapers, but the full circumstances have not, as yet, been given at one time. O'Connell, the greatest orator, as well as the greatest lawyer and logician that Ireland ever produced, was initiated into Freemasonry in 1799 in Lodge 189, Dublin, of which he became Master in the following year. It is said that no one ever carried out the duties of his office with more brilliant success than he, who himself acknowledged that he felt deeply interested in his Masonic work, which was proved plainly by his unceasing activity. O'Connell was standing counsel to the Grand Lodge of Ireland in some tedious litigation caused by an unscrupulous Grand Secretary and the Irish Rolls bears his signature under date of 24th July, 1813, as Counsel representing the Grand Lodge of Ireland. Bro. William White, who was Deputy Grand Master of Ireland from 1830 to 1840, used to declare with pride that he had received his degrees at the hand of the great liberator. It is easy to conceive with what skill a man so highly gifted as he was would perform his work and how attentively the brethren would listen to that fascinating voice which bewitched the Courts of Justice and the Senate. In addition to his membership of his Mother Lodge, he was founder of a lodge in Trales, of which he became the first Senior Warden and a joining member of Lodge No. 13, Limerick. He afterwards withdrew from all his lodges because of the enforcement of the Papal Bull in Ireland and, on 19th April, 1837, the following letter from his pen appeared in the "Pilot" newspaper of London:

"To the Editor of the 'Pilot:'

"Sir, - A paragraph has been going the rounds of the Irish newspapers purporting to have my sanction, and stating that I had been at one time Master of a Masonic lodge in Dublin and still continue to belong to that society.

"I have since received letters addressed to me as a Freemason and feel it incumbent on me to state the real facts.

"It is true that I was a Freemason and a Master of a lodge. It was at a very early period of my life and either before ecclesiastical censure had been published in the Catholic Church in Ireland prohibiting the taking of the Masonic oaths, or, at least, before I was aware of that censure. I now wish to state that, having become acquainted with it, I submitted to its influence and many, very many, years ago unequivocally renounced Freemasonry. I offered the late Archbishop, Dr. Troy, to make that renunciation public, but he deemed it unnecessary. I am not sorry to have this opportunity of doing so.

"Freemasonry in Ireland may be said to have (apart from its oaths) no evil tendency, save as far as it may counteract in some degree the exertions of those most laudable institutions - deserving of every encouragement - the temperance societies.

"But the great, the important objection is this - the profane taking in vain the awful name of the Deity - in the wanton and multiplied taking of oaths - of oaths administered on the Book of God, either in mockery or derision, or with a solemnity which renders the taking of them, without any adequate motive, only the more criminal. This objection, which, perhaps, I do not state strongly enough, is alone abundantly sufficient to prevent any serious Christian from belonging to that body.

"My name having been dragged before the public on this subject it is, I think, my duty to prevent any person supposing that he was following my example in taking oaths which I now certainly would not take, and, consequently, being a Freemason, which I certainly would not now be.

"I have the honor to be,

"Your faithful servant,

"Daniel O'Connell."

At the next meeting of the Grand Lodge of Ireland, on the 4th May following, attention was drawn to the letter by Deputy Grand Master White, when two resolutions were proposed, the first that a committee be appointed to take into consideration the letter and to report on the same to a subsequent meeting of the Grand Lodge; the second, or, rather, the amendment, was that the Grand Secretary be instructed to write Mr. Daniel O'Connell to ascertain if he was the author of the letter in question, or, in other words, to make certain of the genuineness of the communication. The amendment was passed by a large majority, and O'Connell's reply to the query of the Grand Secretary was short, but to the point. He merely wrote in his own hand:

"I am the author of the letter above alluded to.

"Daniel O'Connell,

"28th May, 1837."

Thereupon it was proposed, seconded, and carried by the Grand Lodge of Ireland without a division:

"That Brother Daniel O'Connell formerly of Lodge 189 be excluded from all the rights and benefits of Freemasonry," the ground being the misleading character of the letter.

With regard to Dr. Troy, whose name was mentioned in Daniel O'Connell's letter, it has been frequently stated in the public press, particularly of the period at which O'Connell wrote, that Dr. Troy, the Archbishop, and Dr. Tuohy, the Roman Catholic Bishop of Limerick, were both respected members of the Order. The Freemasons Quarterly Review of 1842 said that "it was at a levee at the Duke of Richmond's court, when Lord Lieutenant of Ireland, that the secret was discovered. As Dr. Troy was standing near the vice-regal chair, he happened, by mere accident, to make one of the old-cherished signs which was caught up by another brother, who immediately responded. An introduction took place immediately after and in the course of the conversation which followed, Dr. Troy said, 'You shall ever find me Brother Troy, but not as priest or bishop." The Rev. John Thaer, a native of Boston, U. S. A., formerly a dissenting minister, but afterwards a Roman Catholic priest in Limerick, was also a Freemason.

The publicity given to O'Connell's letter seems to have instigated a series of petty persecutions, or, as they may be appropriately termed, "pinpricks." On 27th March, 1842, to quote one illustration, the parishioners of St. Michael's Roman Catholic Church were, publicly cautioned not to attend the Masonic ball to be held in aid of the Masonic Orphan Charity on the following Thursday "under penalty of exposure and denunciation from the altar" on the following Sunday, when the names of those attending would be duly published.

It was about this time that the Archbishop of Tuam addressed the following letter to the Rev. J.U. McDonough, a Roman Catholic priest in Canada:

"Rev. dear sir: - Having been informed by you that there are in Canada some misguided Catholics who would strive to justify the practices of Freemasonry, scruple not to assert that it was sanctioned by priests and Bishops in Ireland, allow me to tell you that this was never the case; and that these men are only aggravating their disobedience to the Church by the additional guilt of calumny. I have had extensive acquaintance, not only with the present race of ecclesiastics, but also with some of those venerable men of more ancient standing, some of whom are no more, and I can confidently state that neither in this city, nor in any other part of Ireland, was the bond of Masonry sanctioned by any portion of the clergy. That Freemasons' lodges were then more numerous and frequent than now, may be true; but their existence, in contempt and defiance of the repeated denunciations of the clergy, cannot be brought as an argument of their sanction of the same, more than the prevalence of other evils against which they do not cease to raise their voices, could be adduced as a proof of similar connivance."

In 1843, Francis Xavier Carnana, Roman Catholic Archbishop of Rhodes and Bishop of Malta, issued a Pastoral Letter against Freemasonry, which he ordered to be posted on the doors of, and read in, every Roman Catholic Church in Malta. The Letter, which is a vile document and speaks for itself, was as follows:

Nos Don Franciscus Xaverius Carnana, Venerabilibus Fratribus et Dilectis, Capitulo, Clero, Populoque Diocesis Melitensis, salutem in Domino Sempiternam.

"We feel it to be a duty of our pastoral ministry to conceal as much as possible such sins as may be committed by a few persons in secret, so that the bad example of these may not be known to, or followed by, other, to the scandal of the Church and corruption of good manners. Up to this period this policy has been followed by us, for our ecclesiastical doctrine teaches us through the Holy Spirit, to listen for a time silently, and meanwhile search diligently: *audi tacens simul et quaerens.*

We now draw your attention to that iniquitous congregation, that detestable lodge; for we are at a loss by what epithet to denounce a meeting held in a building in an obscure corner of the city of Senglea. After long suffering, we are still grieved to see that the several means which, with evangelical prudence, we have hitherto adopted to overturn and eradicate this pernicious society have proved futile; so that at length we feel ourselves under the necessity of publicly, loudly, and energetically raising our voice to exhort, in the name of our Lord, all our beloved diocesans, to keep far away from this infernal meeting, whose object is nothing less than to loosen every divine and human tie, and to destroy, if possible, the very foundation of the Catholic Church. We also threaten with the thunders of that Church any persons who, unhappily for them, may belong to any secret society, whether as a member, or in any way connected with, helping or favoring, directly or indirectly, such society or any of its acts.

"We, with anguish of heart, heard long ago, almost immediately on its first assemblage, of the creation of this diabolical lodge, and being very desirous that the land under our spiritual dominion (these islands of Malta and Gozo) should continue in ignorance of what was doing under the veil of darkness, in an obscure part of the city of Senglea, by a few ill-advised individuals, and that none of our flock should by chance, or from motives of interest, be tempted to join this pestilential pulpit of iniquity and error - we have as yet only adopted the evangelical advice of secretly warning and admonishing, leaping always that the attacks made on the human and divine laws established among us mislit be foiled, and become harmless; but seeing now, that, in spite of all our silent workings, the meetings of this lodge still continue, we openly, and with all that apostolic frankness, characteristic of the Catholic clergy, in the name of God Almighty, and of His only true Roman Catholic and Apostolic Church, and authorized as we are expressly by the papal authority, denounce, proscribe, and condemn in the most public manner, the instalment, union, meetings, and all the proceedings of this lodge of abominations; as being diametrically opposed to our sacred Catholic religion, as destructive to every celestial law, every mundane authority, contradictory to every evangelical maxim, and as tending to disorganize, put to flight, and utterly destroy whatever of religion, of honesty, and all good there may be in the Holy Catholic Faith, or among our peaceful citizens, under the deceitful veil of novelty, of a badly understood philanthropy, and a specious freedom.

"We therefore believe it to be our duty, most beloved diocesans, to address you under these deplorable circumstances; to incite you to entertain the most profound horror and the deepest antagonism for this lodge, union, or society, which endeavors, although as yet in vain, to vomit hell against, to stigmatize the immaculate purity of our sacred Catholic religion. Its pernicious orgies anticipate the overthrow of that Order which reigns on earth, promote an unbridled freedom of action, unchecked by law, for the gratification of the most depraved and disorderly passions. Do not allow yourselves to be deceived by their seducing language, which proffers humanity fraternal love, but, in reality, tends to discord, universal anarchy, and total ruin, the destruction of all religion, and the subversion of every philanthropic establishment. Their agents industriously hide their malignant intentions by deceitful and never-to-be-redeemed promises. The great solicitude evinced to conceal every action of this society under a mask will make you distrust its word, for honorable undertakings are always manifest and open, courting observation and inquiry; sins and iniquities alone bury themselves in secrecy and obscurity.

"Fathers of families, and you, also, to whom is entrusted the education of youth, be diligent and be careful of your precious charge; see that they be not contaminated by this plague spot, which, although now confined to one domicile, yet threatens to spread the pestilence amongst us; scrutinize the books they read, examine the character of their associates. It is a well-known practice of this secret society to seduce over youth, under the specious pretext of communicating to them, disinterestedly, scientific knowledge. Flee, then, O beloved diocesans, as from the face of a venomous serpent, the society, the very neighborhood of, and all connection with these tutors of impiety, who wish to confound light and darkness, trying, if possible, to obscure the former, and make you embrace and follow the latter. You cannot possibly gain anything good from disturbers of rule and order, who show no veneration for God and His religion, no esteem for any authority, ecclesiastical or civil: - men, deceitful and fashioning, who, under a show of social honesty, and a warm love for their species, are stirring up an atrocious war with all that can render human society honorable, happy and tranquil.

"Consider them as so many pernicious individuals, to whom Pope Leo XII, in his often-repeated Bulls, ordered that none should give hospitality, not even a passing salute.

"Instead of such persons, bring around you honest and just men, who give 'unto God that which is God's and unto Caesar that which is Caesar's,' endeavouring to do their duty to God and to their neighbor.

"Finally, we absolutely prohibit persons of any grade or condition from having any connection with this lodge, from cooperating, even indirectly, in its establishment or extension. We order them to prevent others from frequenting it, or giving to its members a place of meeting, under any pretext. We place every one under an obligation to denounce to us all persons who may belong to this lodge in any capacity, either as members or agents of a secret union, founded by the devil himself.

"Datum Valettae, in Palatio nostro Archiepiscopali, die 14 Octobris, 1843."

It should be explained that the lodge referred to was the Union of Malta, No. 407, which was constituted in Bermola in 1832, although the first minute extant is dated 3rd November, 1840. It was removed to Senglea in 1843, where, as evidenced in the foregoing remarkable epistle, it aroused the ire of the Roman Catholic Bishop. On the publication of Bishop Carnana's Apostolic Letter, the secretary of the lodge wrote to the Chief Secretary of the Malta Government, lodging a formal complaint, in which communication he said:

"We make our proceedings in this matter officially known to you, not as a Fraternity of Freemasons, well knowing that as such we are not recognized by the government, but as British subjects entitled to be protected by the law from molestation."

The following communication was also sent to the Grand Secretary of England:

"Dear Sir and Brother:- The Right Reverend the Roman Catholic Archbishop of Rhodes and Bishop of Malta, Don Francis Scaverius Carnana, having recently issued a pastoral, the object of which was to prohibit and suppress the meetings of Freemasons and other secret societies, and which pastoral is more particularly directed against the Union Lodge, 588 established at Senoea, one of the suburbs of Valetta, Malta, holding their warrant from the United Grand Lodge of London:

"A meeting of the brothers was held at their lodge on Monday, the 13th instant, when the following resolutions were unanimously passed:

"1st. That in consequence of the publication of a pastoral by the Roman Catholic Bishop of Malta on the 14th ultimo, tending to bring into disrespect the Masonic body and endeavour to suppress their meetings, it is imperiously necessary to appeal to the United Grand Lodge in London for such assistance and aid as the circumstances of the case may, in their opinion, call for.

"2nd. That the original document, if procurable, together with a translation of the same, be forwarded to the Worshipful Pro Grand Master, for his perusal, with as little delay as possible.

"3rd. That, knowing the feelings of her Majesty's Judges to be opposed to, the proceedings of Freemasons, no attempt at redress shall be sought in the Malta courts of law.

"In pursuance of the above resolutions, we beg to forward for the perusal of the Worshipful Pro Grand Master copy of the original document, and a translation of the same, praying that effectual assistance from him which the case so manifestly urges.

"By order of the W. M., at the united request of the officers and brethren of the Malta Union Lodge, No. 588.

"E. Goodenough,

"Acting Secretary.

"To Brother Wm. White G.S.,

"United Grand Lodge of England, London.

"Malta, 15th November, 1843,

The answers to those communications have hot, however, been placed on record.

Although in his Encyclical Letter, *Qui pluribus*, dated 9th November, 1846, Pope Pius IX did, not refer to the Freemasons by name; it is undoubtedly to that body that his fulminations are directed when he says:

"For you already know, Venerable Brethren, that there are other deceits and frightful errors with which the children of this age contend against the Catholic religion, and the divine authority and regulations of the Church, and endeavour to trample under foot all laws, as well of the Church as of the State. Such is the tendency of those wicked enterprises which have been undertaken against this Roman See of Blessed Peter, in which Christ laid the impregnable foundation of His Church. Such is the aim of those secret societies which have emerged from their obscurity to devastate and destroy all that is most venerable, both in the Church and in the State, and which have been repeatedly anathematized and condemned by the Roman Pontiffs, our predecessors, in Apostolic Letters, which anathemas, in the plentitude of our Apostolic authority, confirm and command to be diligently obeyed."

It is interesting to know that these "secret societies" are in this Encyclical Letter placed on the same level of iniquity as "those most crafty Bible Societies, which, reviving the old device of the heretics, do not cease to put forth an immense number of copies of the books of the Sacred Scriptures, printed in various vulgar tongues, and often filled with false and perverse interpretations, contrary to the rules of the Holy Church, which they continually circulate at an immense expense and force upon all sorts of persons."

It is interesting to note that, notwithstanding the many Papal Bulls and Encyclicals, the register of the Grand Orient of Lusitania has the names of the Archbishop of Evora and D. Januaire, Bishop-elect of Castello Branco, as being present on the occasion of the election of a successor to the Comte de Tomar, Grand Master.

The Popes, from the time of Leo XII have condemned all secret societies, but, apparently, despite the specific character of the condemnation, this prohibition did not extend to societies limited in membership to members of the Roman Catholic Church, or formed for the propagation of aims sanctioned directly or indirectly by the authorities of that Church. 'History records the formation of many such societies, originating after the date of the first sweeping condemnation. About 1850, or earlier, there was formed in Portugal a secret society which was called the Order of St. Michael of Ala. This Order, according to the first article of its Statutes was essentially secret, militant, and political. It had for its aim, according to its articles, the maintenance of the Catholic, Apostolic, and Roman faith, and the restoration of the Portuguese legitimacy. One of its political means of action was recourse to arms when necessary. Its members took an oath or obligation to preserve inviolably the secrets of the members and the things done in and out of lodge. The Order consisted of several degrees: Novices, Chevaliers, Commanders, Grand Crogs, Master, and Grand Master. Each group of Novices, with its Chevalier, formed a College; a group of Chapters, with a Commander, formed a Chapter; a group of Chapters, with a Grand Cross, formed a Province, of which the Masters and Grand Master were the Superiors. This elaborate constitution notwithstanding the fact that the Popes and Catholics generally accuse Freemasonry of being secret and say to Freemasons, "If the acts which you practice in association are innocent, why do you stipulate for secrecy?" Or, as Dr. Cullen, in his Lenten Pastoral of 1859, said: "As secret societies are the cause of the greatest evils to religion, tending to promote impiety and incredulity, and are most hostile to the public good, the Catholic Church has solemnly excommunicated all her children who engage in them. Hence, no Catholic can be absolved who is a Freemason, a Ribbonman, or enrolled in any other secret society."

On the 11th February, 1857, at a meeting of the Grand Lodge of England, presided over by the Earl of Zetland, Grand Master, the Earl of Carnarvon moved: "That the Grand Lodge having seen with regret the antagonistic position assumed by the Roman Catholic Church towards Masonry, desires the Board of General Purposes to draw up a statement of the principles of the Order, that the same may be sent to the Masters of all lodges under the Grand Lodge of England in Roman Catholic countries, to be used by them as they shall think fit." After much discussion, however, the motion was negatived, and if comment may be made upon the outcome, may it not be said that the negative decision was a wise one. The Earl of Carnarvon, however, speaking at Stonehouse the following month, said that at Malta, the Mauritius, Trinidad, and Hong Kong Freemasons had been deprived of their civil and religious privileges and had been interdicted from baptism, marriage, and burial by the Roman Catholic clergy.

In 1857, Freemasonry was introduced into the Republic of Ecuador by the Grand Orient of Peru, which organized lodges in Guayaquil and Quito. Three years later, the Dictator, Garcia Moreno, sought admission into the Fraternity. His application was refused on account of his notoriously immoral character; and, in revenge, he called in the Jesuits, who ruthlessly suppressed all the lodges. Moreno was assassinated in 1875, but twelve months elapsed before the population were able to shake off the oppressive yoke of the priesthood.

CHAPTER VI

ON SEPTEMBER 25th, 1865, a further fulmination against the Freemasons was launched by the Roman Pontiff, Pius IX, an Allocution delivered in a Secret Consistory, the document being known from its first two words, Multiplices inter. It was worded as follows:

"Venerable Brethren: Among the numerous machinations and artifices by which the enemies of the Christian name have tried to attack the Church of God, and sought to shake and besiege it by efforts superfluous in truth, must undoubtedly be reckoned the perverse society of men called Masonic, which at first confined to darkness and obscurity, now comes into light for the common ruin of religion and human society. Immediately that our predecessors, the Roman Pontiffs, faithful to their pastoral office, discovered its snares and frauds, they considered there was not a moment to lose in holding in check by their authority, and in striking and lacerating by an admonitory sentence as with a sword, this sect pursuing crime and attacking holy and public things. Our predecessor, Clement XII, by his Apostolic Letters, proscribed and rebuked this sect, and dissuaded all the faithful not only from joining it but also from promoting or encouraging it in any manner whatever, since such an act would entail the penalty of excommunication, which the Roman Pontiff can alone remove. Benedict XIV confirmed by his Constitution this just and legitimate sentence of admonition and did not fail to exhort the Catholic Sovereign Princes to devote all their effort and all their solicitude to repress this most immoral sect, and defend society against a common danger. Would to God these monarchs had listened to the words of our predecessor! Would to God that in so serious a matter they had acted less feebly! In truth, neither we nor our fathers would then have had to deplore the many seditious movements, the many incendiary wars which have set the whole of Europe in flames, nor the many bitter misfortunes which have afflicted and still afflict the Church. But the rage of the wicked being far from appeased, Pius VII, our predecessor, struck with anathema the sect of recent origin, Carbonarism, which had propagated itself, particularly in Italy, and inflamed by the same zeal for souls, Leo XII condemned, by his Apostolic Letters, not only the secret societies we have just mentioned, but all others, of whatever appellation, conspiring against the Church and the civil power, and warned all the faithful to avoid them under penalty of excommunication. Nevertheless, these efforts of the Apostolic See have not had the success expected. The Masonic sect of which we speak has not been vanquished or overthrown; on the contrary, it has so developed itself that in these troublous days it exists everywhere with impunity, and carries an audacious front. We have, therefore, thought it our duty to return to this matter, since, perhaps from ignorance of the guilty intrigues clandestinely carried on, an erroneous opinion may arise that the character of this society is inoffensive, that its institution has another object than that of succoring men, and assisting them in adversity, and that in this society there is no need to fear for the Church of God. But should this not comprehend how this sect departs from the truth? What is the object of this association of men belonging to all religions and every belief ? To what end these clandestine meetings, and the rigorous oath exacted from the initiate, binding them never to reveal anything of what may be discussed? Wherefore that unheard of atrocity of penalties and chastisements which the initiated bind themselves to accept should they fail to keep their oath? A society which thus avoids the light of day must surely be impious and criminal. 'He who does ill,' says the apostle, 'hates the light.' How different from such an association are the pious societies of the faithful which flourish in the Catholic Church! With them there is no reticence, no obscurity. The law which governs them is clear to all; clear also are the works of charity practised according to the gospel doctrine. Thus it is not without grief that we have seen Catholic societies of this nature, so consolatory and so well calculated to excite piety and succor the poor, attacked and even destroyed in some places, while, on the contrary, encouragement is afforded to secret Masonic societies, so inimical to the Church of God, so dangerous even for the security of kingdoms.

"Venerable Brethren, we feel pain and bitterness to see that when it is requested to rebuke this sect according to the constitutions of our predecessors, some persons show themselves indulgent, almost supine; whereas, in so grave a matter, the exigencies of their functions and their charges demand that they should display the greatest activity. If these persons think that the Apostolic Constitutions, fulminated under penalty of anathema against occult sects and their adepts and abettors, have no force in the countries where the said sects are tolerated by the civil power, they are assuredly very greatly in error. As you are aware, Venerable Brethren, we have already rebuked, and now anew rebuke and condemn, the falsity of this evil doctrine. In fact, can it be that the supreme power of pastoring and guiding the universal flock which the Roman pontiffs received from Christ in the person of the Blessed Teacher, and the supreme power they must exercise in the Church, should depend upon the civil power, or could they for any reason be constrained and done violence to thereby? Under these circumstances, for fear lest youth and unthinking men should allow themselves to be led astray in principle, and for fear our silence should offer any opportunity of protecting error, we have resolved, Venerable Brethren, to raise our apostolic voice, and confirming here in your presence the constitutions of our predecessors, on part of our apostolic authority we rebuke and condemn this Masonic society and the other societies of the same description, which, although differing in form, tend to the same end, and which conspire overtly or clandestinely, against the Church or legitimate power. We desire that the said societies should be held proscribed and rebuked by us, under the same penalties as those which are specified in the previous constitutions of our predecessors, and this in the sight of all the faithful in Christ, of every condition, rank, and dignity, and throughout all the earth. There remains now nothing wanting to satisfy the wishes and solicitude of our paternal heart than to warn and admonish the faithful who should have associated themselves with sects of this character to obey in the future wiser inspirations, and to abandon these fatal counsels, in order that they may not be dragged into the abyss of eternal perdition. As regards all others of the faithful, if they wish solicitude for their souls we strongly exhort them to be upon their guard against the perfidious language of sectarians, who, under a fair exterior, are inflamed with a bunting hatred against the religion of Christ and legitimate authority, and who have but one single thought and single end, viz., to overthrow all rights, both human and divine. Let them well understand that those affiliated to such sects are like the wolves which Christ our Lord prophesied would come disguised in sheep's clothing to devour the flock; let them understand they are of the number of those whose society the apostle has also forbidden to us, eloquently prohibiting us from even saying unto them - Hail!

"May the All-Merciful God, hearing our prayers, grant that with the aid of His grace the insensate may return to reason, and those who have gone astray be led back to the path of justice. May God grant that after the suppression of the depraved men, who, by the aid of the above-mentioned societies, give themselves up to impious and criminal acts, the Church and human society may be able to repose in some degree from such numerous and inveterate evils!

"In order that our vows may be heard, let us also pray to our Mediatrix with the All-Clement God, the Most Holy Virgin, that Mother Immaculate from her birth, to whom it has been granted to overthrow the enemies of the Church and monstrous errors. Let us equally pray for the protection of the blessed apostles, Peter and Paul, by whose glories built this noble city has been sanctified. We have confidence that with their assistance and aid we shall the more easily obtain what we ask of the Divine bounty."

It is problematical whether Pope Pius IX would not have stayed his hand, or his pen, if he had possessed the foreknowledge of the storm of criticism, satire, derision, and ridicule which his puerile denunciation aroused in all sections of the public press throughout the land, but infallibility is not a term inclusive of foreknowledge. Courteous attention is always accorded the opinions of the heads of all religious bodies by the members of the "fourth estate," even when they travel beyond the bounds of reason, but here there was a general consensus of opinion that, in common parlance, the Pope had made himself "look silly," and many papers did not hesitate to express this opinion in the plainest possible language.

The Times in a leading article wrote:

"The telegraph informed us a few days ago, as much to our surprise as to our satisfaction, that the Pope, in Secret Consistory, had delivered an allocution denouncing all secret societies, and particularly the Freemasons and the Fenians. Although we knew that the Roman Catholic clergy were uniformly hostile to the Fenian movement, we could hardly have expected that the Pope himself would come forward with such vigor and promptitude to render us a service at such an opportune moment. The text of this unexpected allocution has now reached us, and will be found today in another column of our impression. It will be seen that though it does not denounce the Fenians by name, it is directed against all secret societies 'by whatsoever name called, which conspire against the Church and civil power.' There have been few secret societies which answer to this description more exactly than the Fenians; and the Roman Catholic clergy, it has been amply proved, had as much reason as any other class of the community to assist in the suppression of this disorderly brotherhood. We may, therefore, congratulate ourselves on having for once the cordial assistance of the Pope in our Irish policy. We cannot but be very much obliged to so exalted a personage for thus going out of his way to support us against the machinations of Mr. Stephens and Mr. John O'Mahoney. We are, indeed, somewhat afraid that these conspirators and their American allies will derive more satisfaction from the dignity of being by implication made the subjects of a Papal allocution than they will be afflicted by the tremendous denunciations which are launched against them. Nevertheless, it cannot but be well, as far as it goes, that the head of the Roman Catholic Church should have formally supported his subordinates in denouncing these foolish and wicked conspiracies. Our New York correspondent lately informed us that among the extraordinary hallucinations of Fenianism in America was a rumor that a special order had been issued from Rome, expressed in true papal Latin *Fenianos non esse inquietandos.* If anything can disabuse an Irishman of a favorite delusion, or induce an American to relinquish a smart fabrication, the rumor in question ought to be effectually dispersed by this papal thunderbolt.

"But in thus expressing our acknowledgments to the Pope for his well-intentioned services, we must, at the same time, indulge our surprise at the main purport of the document before us. The denunciation of Fenianism is, as we have said, only implied incidentally. The Papal thunders are more immediately directed against a very different society; and if the allocution is to have any effect it will somewhat diminish the satisfaction with which we receive it that it consigns to perdition, along with the Fenians, all the members of a society which is as numerous in England as in Ireland, and which spreads its ramifications over almost every country in the world. This unhappy society is none other than that of the Freemasons. 'Among the many machinations,' says the Pope, 'by which the enemies of the Christian name have dared to assail the Church of God, to destroy and sap it by methods alien from the truth, must doubtless be reckoned that wicked association of men called Masonic.' Such an alarming exordium will probably be as surprising to the Freemasons as to every one else; but it is only an appropriate introduction to the vehement denunciations which follow. Freemasonry is a 'dark society - the enemy of the Church and of God, and dangerous even to the security of kingdoms.' If Freemasons do not give up their 'wicked assemblies' they must expect to be 'hurried along into the abyss of eternal ruin.' They 'are kindled with an ardent hatred against the religion of Christ and legitimate authority.' They are the wolves in sheep's clothing of whom it is predicted in the Gospel that they would come to devour the flock. They have lost their reason, their acts are 'impious and criminal' and their errors 'monstrous.' The Popes, it appears, have long ago detected their snares and deceptions, and one after another have resolved, 'without losing a moment' to 'strike and lacerate with a sentence of excommunication as with a sword this sect breathing crime and attacking civil and sacred life.' No fewer than four pontiffs appear to have launched their thunders against these enemies of all enemies of all justice and religion, and nothing can exhibit the intense iniquity of the society in a stronger light than that it has survived these excommunications and in these distressed days everywhere shows itself and lifts its audacious front.' The paternal heart, therefore, of the present Pope compels him to suppress these wicked men and relieve society from such enormous and inveterate evils; and terrible are the punishments which he threatens for this benevolent purpose. In the first place, all the Freemasons are in danger of eternal ruin, and all the other faithful must refuse them any countenance if they would avoid sharing their fate. They are to be interdicted from all Christian society, for the Pope assures us that they are the very persons with whom the apostle forbids us to eat, or so much as to exchange salutation. Finally, the divine aid, and that of the Virgin and the Apostles, is solemnly invoked, and the Pope concludes by expressing his conviction that with such assistance he shall succeed in extirpating this abominable association.

"We cannot but ask ourselves in simple astonishment - what does all this mean? Is the Pope inspired or frenzied, or is he merely practising his Latin so as to keep his hand in for the Emperor Napoleon when he commences the withdrawal of his troops from Rome? The Pope, we know, in Secret Consistory, talks neither English nor any other modern language, and it may be that this astonishing fulmination is only his way of saying that he disapproves of Freemasonry. We are all more or less familiar with the Freemasons. We know that they have an elaborate organization, and call each other long names, that they wear upon occasions very strange aprons, that they preserve certain antiquated ceremonies, and, above all, that they give very good balls and excellent dinners, and are generally a very hospitable and liberal set of men. We know, again, that the Freemasons profess to take certain solemn oaths, and to be in possession of some secrets which explain the whole mystery of political society upon architectural principles, or something equally magnificent. But as to assertions that they devote themselves to 'unheard-of atrocities of penalties and chastisements in case they should break their oath,' we feel pretty sure the Pope must be misinformed. We have never observed that they were oppressed by any such weight as would necessarily hang over their minds if they were at all times conscious that a single inadvertence would expose them to such tremendous danger. It would require, in fact, even in a Roman Catholic, a very strong faith in the infallibility of the Pope to accept his description of this Society. Indeed, we sincerely condole with the Roman Catholics if they are to be absolutely debarred, for the future, from enjoying Masonic hospitality. Must the faithful, as a French journal inquires, immediately cut their Masonic friends, and refuse them even a distant bow? Freemasons, so far as we know anything about them, are neither revolutionists nor atheists. If we are not mistaken, Lord Palmerston himself is one of their number, and the late Marshal Magnan, one of the pillars of the new French regime, was the head of the Order in France. What can the Pope be thinking of to select this innocent and convivial association for these tremendous denunciations? If he had simply consigned all the Fenians, in so many words, to eternal perdition unless they, immediately repented and revoked their wicked errors before the nearest priest, the allocution might have appeared to possess some point, some justification. But what have the Freemasons done to provoke such a demonstration? It is said that the Archbishop of Paris lately gave great offence at Rome by attending the funeral of Marshal Magnan. The Archbishop was probably profoundly ignorant of the wicked devices of the Marshal and his fellow Masons, and ordinary observers must avow themselves equally in the dark. In truth, it reminds us of Jupiter thundering in a clear sky, to witness these rattling thunderbolts let loose upon so unobtrusive a society as the Freemasons. Jupiter, like Homer, must, we suppose nod sometimes, and the Secret Consistory must, one would think, have gone to sleep, and this allocution must have been delivered and have been listened to in a dream.

"We have, in short, often had occasion to remark, that the Papacy is either greatly above or greatly below the level of common sense. In the present instance, we have not much hesitation in deciding in which category the papal allocution is to be placed. We can only explain such an uncalled for burst of pontifical wrath on the supposition that the Pope is profoundly ignorant of the circumstances of modern life and society. In Italy, indeed, where the excessive jealousy of the Church tends to invest even the most innocent combinations of men with a political meaning, it is possible that even Freemasonry may assume some definite character of antagonism to the papal pretensions. But that the Pope can think it worth this violent allocution only proves how completely he is in the dark as to the real influences which are actuating men's minds. It is not Freemasonry, nor any other secret society, which has withdrawn from Catholicism so much of the intelligence of Italy and all Europe, and has robbed the Papacy of its ancient possessions. It is simply that general advance of free thought and of personal liberty which has exposed at once the unfounded character of the papal claims and the injurious nature of their assumptions. Ridiculous, in some respects, as are such exhibitions, it is impossible not to feel a certain melancholy when we behold the Papacy thus fighting in the air. In former days it at least knew in what direction to strike, and its blows were as well aimed as they were vigorously delivered. At the present day it appears to have lost at once its sagacity and its vigor. It is blind to its real danger, and its language is as impotent in its violence as its blows are feeble and misplaced. It lives in the world of four centuries ago, and judges alike of men and of events by a medieval standard. If the Pope could but leave the Vatican for awhile, and place himself in one of the real centres of modern life, in London or Paris, or even in Florence, he would discover at once that he had been living, writing, and speaking entirely in the clouds. Such societies as the Freemasons may have been formidable a few centuries ago, but they are of about as much importance to the course of civil and religious life as any other of the now extinct associations of the middle ages. With a similar blindness to his real position, the Pope is said to be firmly convinced that the French troops will never be withdrawn from Rome, and he obstinately refuses, therefore, to come to terms with the only government which, when that inevitable event takes place, can afford him any effectual protection. He and his Church resemble nothing so much as the city to which they cling. A new world has grown up all around them, and they remain venerable but decaying monuments of an ancient but now overthrown empire. The very foundations of Catholicism are sapped, its temporal and spiritual dominion is passing away, and the Pope vaguely conscious of some impending danger, summonses a Secret Consistory and launches his excommunications against Freemasonry!"

The Liverpool Mercury was even more trenchant in its criticism of this absurd document, and its comments could not have afforded much satisfaction to the Roman Catholics in the northern Midlands. Its leading article on the Bull was as follows:

"The recent papal allocution against the unfortunate Freemasons is one of the very oddest things we have come across for a long time. All of a sudden, without any imaginable why or wherefore, just when the queer but harmless fraternity of Freemasonry is about the very last subject in men's thoughts, the Holy Father comes out with a tremendous volley of anathemas in the best style of ecclesiastical Latinity, against a set of people of whom the world knows nothing worse than they have an uncommonly eccentric way of promoting certain very innocent and laudable objects. When all mankind is thinking about Schleswig-Holstein, or the cattle plague, or the cholera, or President Johnson, or the Fenians, or the bank rate of discount, or the Italian elections, or some other topic of intelligible mundane interest, infallibility flares up into a blaze of holy wrath against a respectable (though rather funny) body of men who are chiefly known by giving good dinners and wearing curious aprons, and who have never been credibly accused of doing or meaning harm to any living creature. What, in the name of all that is rational, is the bother about? What horrid crimes have the Freemasons been perpetrating or meditating? There do happen to be secret societies in the world - our own Fenians, for instance - against which a little papal invective might seem not absolutely out of place; yet His Holiness has not a word to say about Fenianism, unless some remote allusion to it can be faintly detected under one or two of his sonorous generalities. But what have the poor Freemasons done to bring down on their heads this lava torrent of denunciation and abuse? What on earth can it all mean? We are told that our Archbishop Manning, from a loyal wish to do the British Empire a good turn, asked His Holiness to launch a handsome fulmination against the Fenians, and that this Allocution is the result. If so, the Archbishop must be considerably pleased. Can it be that His Holiness has made a mistake, misunderstood the drift of the archiepiscopal suggestion, and hurled his thunders in the wrong quarter?

"We are not going to pause for a reply, for we might have to pause for a long time. We have not the slightest expectation that infallibility will so far condescend to human weakness as to explain its own oracles. All that we are permitted to know is that these Freemasons are the most wicked wretches that ever conspired, in a favorite phrase of the papal vocabulary, to 'violate all laws human and divine.' They are pernicious, perverse, impious, immoral, audacious, criminal, and perfidious, depraved, and all the other ugly adjectives known to allocutionary billingsgate. They 'pursue crime and attack holy things.' They 'give themselves up to impious and criminal acts.' They hold 'fatal councils,' and make it their business to drag others into the same 'abyss of eternal perdition' to which they are hurrying themselves. They have but one single thought and single end, namely 'the overthrow of rights, both human and divine.' They are at the bottom of all the mischief that is and has been in the world for at least a century or two. To their account must be set down the many seditious movements, the many incendiary wars, which have set the whole of Europe in flames, and the many bitter misfortunes which have afflicted and still afflict the Church.' Such is the papal reading of the philosophy of modern history. It is a sin and shame that civil governors should tolerate these implacable foes of all that is good and holy. The venerable pontiff cannot contain himself for rage when he remembers how they and their abettors have been excommunicated over and over again, and yet nobody seems to mind it. Clement XII put them down; and Benedict XIV put them down again; and so did Pius VII; and so did Leo XII; and yet they are not really put down at all, but flourish more exuberantly than ever, 'existing everywhere with impunity and carrying an audacious front.' What can have possessed the 'Catholic sovereign princes' that they have not devoted all their efforts and all their solicitude to repress this immoral sect and defend society against a common danger? However, let it be hoped that Catholic sovereign princes and the faithful generally will be roused at last to a sense of their perils and their duties. Henceforth let it be quite understood that these horrid Freemasons, one and all, are excommunicated, and that their guilt and its punishment are shared by all who 'promote or encourage them in any way.' These wolves in sheep's clothing 'are of the number of those whose society the apostle has forbidden to us, eloquently prohibiting us from saying unto them, Hail!' No true Roman Catholic from this time forward must so much as say, 'How do you do?' to an acquaintance of the aproned fraternity. It really is not quite so clear as one could wish that there would be any particular sin in a true Roman Catholic killing the first Freemason he meets. It is at least certain - as far as infallibility can make it - that the Freemasons are the arch enemies of the Church, religion, law, government, truth, morality, and everything else which men count sacred, and that all the heresies, seditions, revolutions of modern times may be traced to the machinations of this thrice accursed sect. With that stupendous perversity civilized society persists in seeing nothing in Freemasonry but a somewhat fantastic sort of benefit society, organized for purposes of charity and good fellowship!

"This is really imbecility in excelsis. The force of infallible folly surely could no further go than in launching this prodigious piece of ecclesiastical thunder against a body of decent gentlemen, whose 'machinations,' though they may begin (for aught we know) with a droll ceremonial which frightens raw novices half out of their wits, end in nothing more terrible than good cheer and a mutual benevolence fund. The Pope's last is certainly his best. We have had many curious allocutions in our time, but this beats them all. Serious comment on such a heap of stark, raving nonsense is impossible. The spectacle of absurdity in a towering rage, a silliness foaming at the mouth, is one that at once defies and disarms criticism. There is nothing to be said of it except that it is a pity that an ancient institution which has outlived its day cannot make a more respectable preparation for its inevitable end. The temporal power of the papacy is justly doomed as an offence against civilization, a wrong to Italy, and a scandal and hindrance to the very religion whose name it takes in vain; but no chivalrous enemy can desire that it should make itself unnecessarily ridiculous. We sincerely sympathize with those multitudes of enlightened and right-minded Roman Catholics to whom it must be unutterably painful to them to pity a pontiff whom they would fain, if possible, reverence."

The Dublin Evening Mail was no less scathing in its comments. A short leader in that paper said:

"We echo in our columns today the last peal of thunder from the Vatican. It is designed to frighten the Freemasons; but it only makes known the force of the now impotent thunderer. Amid the empty sound and puerile verbiage of this allocution, a whispered confession of real motives tells the tale of the crime of Freemasonry in papal eyes: 'A false opinion may arise that the end of this society is inoffensive, and that this institution has no other end but to succor men and to aid them in adversity, and that the Church has nothing to fear from this society. Who, however, does not understand that this is far from being the truth? What does this association of men of all religions, of all creeds, mean?' It is truly strange that, wrapped up as it may be in any amount of fustian, the secret design of the Vatican heart is never successfully concealed in an allocution. Nothing can be more true than that the papal power has everything to fear from every peaceful and kindly 'association of men of all religions and of all creeds.' It is, therefore, the thunder is directed against a form of association which peculiarly tends to unite men in bonds of charity, mutual tolerance, and good will. The present allocution is, in fact, not merely a denunciation of Freemasons, but a practical comment upon the Roman reading of the divine proclamation of 'Peace on earth, good-will to men.' Pio Nono and his Secret Consistory proclaim, according to their version, 'Peace on earth to men of good-will,' but only to those whose will is good towards the papal system. Carried out to its logical end, the proposal 'to strike and rend' as with a sword 'the Masonic Society' is an anathema against all forms of union or association between men of different creeds - it is an edict of non-intercourse among fellow subjects, kinsmen, friends."

The Gloucestershire Chronicle prophesied an early downfall of the Papacy, based upon an estimation of its apparent effete and decadent condition:

"There are some constitutions," the writer said, "which, when about to break up through old age or some heavy infirmity, betray traces of their earlier vigor by bursting forth at times into paroxysms of passion as impotent as they are ridiculous. This seems to be the case with the Pope, who, some time ago, in a secret consistory held at Rome, delivered an allocution, or, more properly, an anathema, chiefly against the Masonic Society, and also against 'all other societies, of whatever appellation, conspiring against the Church and the civil power.' Europe is rather astounded; it can hardly believe its eyes when the explosive document is thrown before it. Various reasons are assigned for the papal thunder in a clear sky, for the revival of absolute dictation to the governments of the world, as though the spiritual power of the papacy were this day an acknowledged fact, in full supremacy, when the truth is it is nothing more than a feeble voice issuing from a throne both spiritually and temporarily shaken almost to dissolution.

"Some allege the Pope takes this left-handed way of administering a heavy blow to the Emperor of the French, because he is about to withdraw his troops from Rome, and has also countenanced Masonry in France; in this manner revenge the Emperor's withdrawal of his military protection and planting a spiritual thorn in the bosom of his subjects. This has always been the subtle policy of Rome, to make mischief between sovereigns and subjects; she scatters a few religious seeds of discord, and rejoices to set a spiritual at variance with the temporal allegiance. A small spite this, now, especially in our age; but the allocution is full of little cat-spittings, so to speak. Again, it is said, the Archbishop of Paris stands rebuked for having attended the funeral of Marshal Lamoriciere, who was formerly the Grand Master of Freemasonry in France; also that Dr. Manning, being desirous of obtaining the Pope's denial of any sympathy with Fenianism, suggested a denunciation of all secret societies, thus believing the net would be large enough to haul in the Fenians together with Freemasons and Carbonari; lastly, it is stated the allocution is a sort of protest against the decline both of the faith and influence of the Church in Italy, as though the falling-off were to be traced, not to the inherent weakness and corruption of Rome herself, but to the 'perfidious nature of sectarians, who, under a fair exterior, are inflamed with a burning hatred against the religion of Christ and legitimate authority and to have but one single thought and single end, viz., the overthrow of rights both human and divine.' It is possible some truth may underlie every one of the motives thus suggested; at any rate, 'Rome has spoken,' and if all the world attended to Rome's senile mutterings, every Freemason would be excommunicated, in the blessed company of Fenians, Carbonari, bandits, and brigands.

"The holy horror of the Pope at Freemasonry is depicted in very strong language, with a remarkable display of ignorance, and a total unconsciousness of history. He describes it as 'that perverse society of men, vulgarly styled Masonic, which at first confined to darkness and obscurity, now comes into light for the common ruin of religion and human society.' He calls it 'a most immoral sect.' At its door he lays 'the many seditious movements, the many incendiary wars, which have set the whole of Europe in flames; as also the many bitter misfortunes which have afflicted and still afflict the Church.' He speaks tremblingly of 'Clandestine meetings,' 'rigorous oaths,' an unheard-of atrocity of penalties and chastisements to be inflicted upon the perjured Mason; and he winds up with an emphatic conclusion: 'A Society which thus avoids the day must surely be impious and criminal.'

"We could add a few more choice specimens of papal eloquence, but these are sufficient for our purpose, unless, indeed, we might be tempted to give our Masonic readers the opportunity of knowing what a disgusting, outlawed, and excommunicated set of vagabonds they really are, as seen through the infallible microscope. 'Let them well understand that those affiliated to such sects are like wolves, whom Christ our Lord prophesied would come disguised in sheep's clothing to devour the flock; let them understand they are of the number of those whose society the Apostle has also forbidden to us, eloquently prohibiting us from even wishing them god-speed.'

"Now, these are truculent expressions which are sufficient to raise the hair on the head of those benevolent gentlemen - there are thousands of them - who, thinking no harm, sit down to dinner after the labors of the lodge are concluded, and drinkings; a glass of wine to all good brethren scattered over the face of the globe, believe they are friends with the world. What a dreadful portrait has the Pope drawn of them, in revolutionary costume, eager to slay, burn, and destroy! Now, none would imagine after reading the allocution, that at the close of the eighth century, the popes conceded to the Masons of Como the exclusive monopoly of erecting churches; they were associated as a craft or brotherhood; they were invested by papal bulls with extensive privileges; they were subject only to their own laws, and were untaxed. 'The lodges of the north' built Strasbourg and Cologne cathedrals; they were encouraged and protected by ecclesiastical authority; Europe abounds with their labors, and the marks of their secret craft are still upon the stones, just as they are Masonically accepted this day. William of Wykeham and Waynefleet, both Bishops, were Grand Masters in England; several of our own Bishops, both past and present, have been Masters of lodges. What then becomes of the Pope's history, and of what force are his denunciations? Masonry has always remained the same; its principles are unchanged; the symbolical teachings were the same in the Como lodges as they are this day in London; the secrets are the same; the ceremonies are identical. The simple fact is, when the Masons ceased to be working societies, and were unnecessary for building churches, Rome threw Masonry on one side, like a useless glove. More than this, Rome will never suffer any intellectual movement over which she has lost the control. But Masonry laid down the trowel and the hod, practically, and confined itself to the speculatively teaching, which was once marvelously united to every stone in building; then the Church of Rome quarrelled with the institution because it presumed to work out a system of morality and religion upon the same foundation of revelation with the Church, but quite distinct from the Church, yet in agreement with the fundamental doctrines of the Church, at the same time not interfering with any Mason's allegiance to the Church. The cause of offence was that this was done without consulting or admitting any ecclesiastical authority. This is the secret of Rome's unmitigated hatred of Masonry; it is her insatiable desire to govern the whole machine of thought and action by priestly hands; while justice and inquisitors exist, the Pope can scarcely with a grave face inveigh against clandestine meetings, rigorous oaths, and the atrocity of penalties and chastisements! We are as certain that the monstrosities imputed by the Pope to Freemasonry are as false as that Freemasons have anything to fear from the Virgin Mary, 'to whom,' says the Pope, It has been granted to overthrow the enemies of the Church and monstrous errors'; or that the Pope will be 'protected by the blessed apostles, Peter and Paul, in his crusade against Freemasonry.' One great principle of Freemasonry is not to interfere with the peculiar religious forms of belief professed by any of its members; armed with this neutrality the Freemason will listen without hatred to the invocation of saints to come down and extinguish the institution; he will only be sorry that such an excess of mistaken zeal should be so uncharitably exercised; for we read in the newspapers the assemblies of Freemasons are already disturbed by ignorant Roman Catholic mobs, who are ready to back the Pope's mild language with any amount of physical assistance.

We know a considerable amount of prejudice exists against Freemasonry even in this country, perhaps chiefly because feminine curiosity remains unsatisfied, or because an exclusive law shuts out the public. For its harmlessness and innocence we might summon the testimony of the many eminent characters in the world who have sanctioned its proceedings from manhood to old age with their countenance; for its benevolence, we can only point to the noble charities sustained from year to year with unostentatious munificence; for its influence we can appeal to the friendly understanding among Masons, and to their kindly offices one towards another. We are told by those who have pursued the real symbolical science of Masonry that it is a fascinating study, demanding the fullest exercise of the mental faculties; that it applies the old scriptural system of instruction by emblem and figure to the acquisition of moral and scientific truths, which are grouped together, engage the memory and captivate the imagination. This, we believe, is the real work of Masonry, and, no doubt, where people have the requisite gifts, nothing can be more lofty or improving, but, in the absence of such qualities, the general body of Masons is content with superficial knowledge; the brethren know enough to come in and out of the lodge, they are ready with their money for any emergency; they will give to good fellowship; there is a freedom of thought which delights them when they are confident they are speaking in the bosom of the family where there is no skeleton and no misinterpretation of the language used. This is the English aspect of Freemasonry - a set of open-hearted, good-humored, charitable fellows, brimming over with benevolence, thinking no evil, somewhat mystified with signs and words, but on the whole merry and wise. How different from the Pope's idea! Slouched hats, dark clothes, daggers, manifestos shrouded in vapor, conspirators deadly against popes, and kings and saints, and churches."

The scathing and adverse comments were by no means limited to English newspapers. Much space could be occupied with extracts from various foreign newspapers on the Pope's allocution, but two only must suffice. La Siecle wrote:

"A million of our fellow-citizens are struck with the most terrible engine which the representative of God upon earth can dispose of. It is true they perform their ordinary business just the same as though interdicted from fire and water. The worst that can happen to them is that they cannot be sponsors if they should be asked to do so; but this is an occasion which does not often present itself, and they may find consolation in the circumstance that it will save them the cost of comfits. What interest can the Church of Rome have in thus exposing the impotence of its spiritual chastisements and the complete indifference with which modern society hears the rumbling of the Church's thunder? What man will give up the title of Freemason, or who will hesitate to become a member of a lodge, through fear of excommunication? The era of these papal thunder peals has passed, and the Papacy should renounce these miserable parodies of the past which had its grandeur."

More expository from the Masonic point of view was the criticism of the *New York Reporter* in which paper the following article appeared:

"Freemasonry has been denounced and suspected, in consequence of its being a secret Order. Secrecy in all things, where secrecy is maintained, is not only consistent with innocence, but is also imperatively enforced by necessity, as well as demanded by every consideration of policy. The direct benefits flowing from Masonry are, of course, intended for, and should be participated in, only by its members - by those who have been regularly initiated into its mysteries and contribute to its support. They are secured by a knowledge of universal language, which is used as a test of brother-hood. This universal language (universal to Masons) is, under no circum-stances, communicated to the world at large. The words and signs of it are secret; for to communicate them would at once destroy its utility. And, strange as it may seem to the uninitiated, our Society professes to have no secrets beyond these. There is little, very little, in the lodge to gratify the eye of the inquisitive. We do not tempt them with offers to unfold some mighty mystery; we can impart to them no superhuman wisdom; we possess not the elixir of life, nor the philosopher's stone, nor the spells of the Tarshun; we cannot and do not profess to be bound by any ties but such as are consis-tent with our duty towards ourselves and families, our neighbors, our coun-try, and our God.

"About the general end of lodge transactions, every one can know as much, as any of its members; but fear of any apprehension on this subject, we would briefly state that nowhere are order and decorum more strictly enforced than in our lodges; our business there is charity and brotherly com-munion, the admission of candidates, and the transaction of such other mat-ters as necessarily pertain to every association. Now, all this is of such a character, that it may with great propriety be kept to ourselves. We are brothers - members of a large family - met for the purpose of transacting our own business, with which the world has no concern; and why should the world be permitted to witness its disposition? Does a needy brother receive assistance, it is not for us to vaunt it, and it might not be agreeable to him to proclaim his wants before strangers, or to have the fact of his being relieved published; and it would certainly be impolitic and uncharitable, by public-ity, to trammel the discussion of character; and how could the announce-ment of the rejection of candidates for our confidence be otherwise than prejudicial to us, by exciting enmity and dissatisfaction in the world. We seek not coalition with the world, made up of a thousand creeds; our objects are few, and their pursuit is quiet and secret; and we have, as Masons, naught in common with the mass of mankind. We do not meddle with politics, nor the extension of the creed by proselytism; we seek only to cultivate the so-cial virtues among ourselves, to benefit each other by deeds of love, and indirectly to benefit the world by our own improvement."

CHAPTER VII

IMMEDIATELY on the publication of the allocution the following circular was addressed by the Heidelberg lodge, Rupprecht zu den funf Rosen, to its sister lodges:

"Venerable and beloved Brethren, —

Doubtless you have all taken cognizance of the allocution addressed on the 25th September by His Holiness Pope Pius IX to the Cardinals assembled in Rome. You know that in this address our Institution is condemned and our Catholic Brethren threatened with the excommunication of the Church. This is not the first time that the Roman Catholic pontiff has launched his thunderbolts against our ancient Order. Clement XII did so on the 28th April, 1738, and Benedict XIV confirmed and amplified the fiat of his predecessors in the Bull of 18th March, 1517. Pius VII and Leo XII have done likewise and with the same want of success as deplored by the present Pope.

"These decrees of the see of Rome have no similarity with the findings of the courts of law. They originate in secret denigrations of which no notice is given to the accused. There is no public prosecution and no opportunity afforded for defence, either public or private. All guarantees for impartial jurisdiction and an unbiased judgment are wanting. Suspicion stands for evidence, the guilt of the accused rests on conjecture, he is convicted without a hearing. Is it a matter of wonder then if public opinion has no confidence in such decrees and strongly deprecates them?

"The Masonic brotherhood is an association of freemen, subject to the laws of the State in which they are located, but not to any clerical authority, it being no clerical institution and adhering to no church as such. For our federation the papal excommunication is therefore devoid of all binding power; but since the head of the Catholic Church condemns us unheard, we will in our turn, hear and examine the motives on which he grounds his opinion.

"The first and paramount reason put forward by all popes in justification of their edicts of condemnation is the reproach urged against us that Freemasonry unites as brethren men of diverse persuasions and religious sects and that by this, as Benedict XIV has it, 'the purity of the Catholic religion is contaminated.'

"The first and main grave charge of all brethren, let us avow it, is true and well-founded. If it be a crime for men of diverse creeds to assemble in peace and harmony, and hold friendly and affectionate communications, irrespective of their religious persuasions, we own and plead guilty to this crime. It is certainly true that our Institution has, from its very beginning, and as it has progressed with increasing determination, professed that there are in all creeds to be found good and honorable men, well adapted to respect and love each other as brethren. In all times Freemasonry considered

70

as a crime and violation of humanity the persecution of man on account of his religious dissension; indeed, every good and true Mason appreciates much more the man who acts up to his moral duty than he who merely professes the most orthodox tenets. But, these doctrines which, for a long time had to be kept secret and harbored in the lodges alone, have become patent, and, in spite of all admonitions of clerical zealots, they are by this time adopted and adhered to by men of education all over the globe, and embodied in the laws of all civilized nations. Should Masonry be condemned on such grounds, the whole civilized world and all cultivated peoples must participate in this condemnation.

"Thank God, a papal thunderbolt issuing from such foundation will produce no destructive effects but it will serve to disclose the nocturnal darkness of intolerance that has procreated it - it will show the world how very backward Rome is in the moral progress of mankind.

"The second head on which the Bull of Benedict XIV is based is the mystery on which our confederation is encircled; indeed, the mystery to which we pledge ourselves has at all times evoked much suspicion, and been a pretext for misinterpretation. But you know how many gross misunderstandings it has given rise to, unfortunately not outside the circle of our Brotherhood only. Still neither the doctrines nor the objects of the Craft are occult, neither its existence - nor are its adherents or their places of meeting unknown nowadays; the signs of recognition alone must remain secret, that the brethren may the more readily distinguish each other abroad, and the internal labors of the lodge must be private that personal confidence may develop itself more fully, and opinions may be uttered more freely. The calm and personal action of the Confederation and the character and moral life of its members, necessitates this precaution. But is it otherwise in the Catholic Church? Is confession public or private? Are the doors of religious and monastic orders and authorities thrown open to the public during their proceedings? Has not every family, every circle of intimate friends, every social club and association secrets of its own? Perhaps, brethren, our lodges are somewhat too strict in this respect, in an age that is very partial to publicity. But surely, such timid solicitude can never be branded as a crime that bears within itself its condemnation.

"The old Masonic oath, with its commination full of grave penalties, was Benedict XIV's third motive for the excommunication of Freemasons, and in this also Pius IX joins his intolerant predecessor. You are aware, brethren, that this formula has been obsolete for a long time past, and is communicated to novices merely as a historical fact belonging to a period that no longer exists. You know that we trust more in the plain word of an honest man than in exaggerated oaths, that are liable to hit up imagination and cool down reason. The third count, therefore, which was never very material, has but an illusory existence with us at the present day.

"As a fourth motive, Benedict XIV quotes the Roman law, by which all associations and corporations are declared illegal which have not obtained the previous acquiesence of the civil authority. But this has nothing to do with the right of the Church. Most civilized governments that are alone called upon to decide in this matter have tolerated and opposed no restrictions on the existence of our Order, before they ever recognized general liberty of association, which is not impugned by the Roman code of laws.

"The fifth motive alleged, viz., the fact of several governments having prohibited the Order, will collapse by itself. Whenever prohibitions of Freemasonry are decreed (and this is done but exceptionally) it is the duty of the lodges to dissolve forthwith, and prove thereby their obedience to the law of the land.

"Benedict XIV alleged as his last motive that many wise and honest men entertain an unfavorable opinion of this Federation. Forsooth, the Pope of Rome should be the last person in the world to base a condemnation on such a ground. No doubt, there is many a wise and honest man who entertains an unfavorable opinion of religious orders and monasteries, nay, of the whole Roman hierarchy.

"Of all the counts of the charge quoted, the first alone is true and material; but the same grounds upon which the Pope curses us constitutes our highest glory in the eyes of the civilized world.

"Now, referring to the latest papal ebullition, Pius IX complains of the inactivity of the Bishops who, he thinks, have proved forbearing and meek in carrying out the papal excommunication, and of the Catholic sovereigns who refrained from suppressing the Association by force; nay, he even accused heaven of having permitted such toleration on the part of the temporal rulers. His strictures on Freemasonry are far more poignant than those of his predecessors. It is true the Roman hierarchs have at no time been at a loss for expressions of violent abuse; but the present edict of Pius IX surpasses all former maledictions by the passionate irruptions of bile it denotes. This we must consider as a further proof of the baneful influence our worst and most uncompromising enemies, the Jesuits, have acquired over the mind and judgment of one whom we believe to be a good-natured Pope.

"Our Federation he calls a criminal sect, although no other 'crime' but human toleration is proved against us, and an immoral sect, though the moral law is essentially the vital principle of Freemasonry. The kindling of revolutions and desolating wars he lays at our door, though every one is fully aware that the commotions and wars in this quarter of the globe originated in forces far different from, and more powerful than, those we commend, and though it is well known that our Association asks of every one of its adherents strict obedience to the laws of the State, that, by virtue of our Constitutions, lodges must abstain from all and every participation in the political struggles of the time, and pursue none but humane and moral objects; that our places of meeting are abodes of peace and neutral ground, the threshold of which the passions of parties are not allowed to cross. The Pope next charges us with entertaining 'growing hatred' towards the Christian religion, although we accept on principle every sincere faith, and the vast majority of brethren profess the religion of Christ, and the moral idea revealed to the world by Christ in His life, as well as in His teachings, cannot possibly be upheld by a moral association but with admiration and veneration. He goes so far as to call us hostile to God, though our prayers are addressed to God, and the whole of our moral strength drawn from the divine and eternal source of human life.

"Let us not follow, brethren, the example of the Roman hierarchy. Let us not return the unjust accusation. We may not oppose our malediction to the course of the Church. Let us pity the sad blindness of the venerable old man whose mind is imposed upon and misled. Let us pray Almighty and Omniscient God to destroy the phantom that has caused the fury of the Pope, and allow his mind to see simple truth, that his curse may be turned into a blessing."

In the course of an article dealing with the allocution and the letter just quoted, the "Deutsche Allgemeine Zeitung" said:

"The Pope has delivered himself of another rude *phillipica* against Freemasonry, that 'reprobate society' and 'criminal sect' that 'aims at nothing but reversion of religion and human society.' It is evidently useless to reason with Rome, which remains eternally the same, and we only wish to remind the Pope that to this 'reprobate society' and 'criminal sect' belong, amongst others, several powerful potentates, as, for example, the King of Prussia. At a time when the last remains of the power of the Pope draw nearer and nearer their final elimination, every friend of intellectual liberty and human progress may hail with delight the allocution that is calculated to accelerate and even secure such 'reversion.'"

At this time also Herr Franz Spiegelthal, Master of the Lodge Zu festen Berg an der Saale of Cable, wrote to the "Freimaurer Zeitung" that the allocution of the Pope had caused him to secede from Roman Catholicism and join the Protestant Church; and, he added, that many of his Catholic friends were likely to follow his example.

In 1869 Cardinal Cullen threatened to excommunicate publicly any Catholics who were found attending a Masonic Ball, and the Earl of Derby, the representative of a family honored for generations among Freemasons, speaking in the House of Lords in the debate on the Irish Church Bill, referring to this threat remarked: "I can only say if his Excellency imagines that the Freemasons of England stand on the same footing with the Carbonari and other secret societies, if he imagines that they are leagued against the throne, that it is a signal proof of the ignorance of infallibility."

On 14th March, 1870, at Madrid, some Roman Catholic priests refused to perform the last sacred rites over the body of Don Enrique de Bourbon because of the presence of certain Masonic emblems on the coffin. On perceiving these the clergy, with one exception, withdrew, taking with them the paraphernalia of their religion. The one remaining priest consented to accompany the body to the cemetery where he performed the funeral ceremony.

In 1871 a pamphlet was published by L'Abbe Joseph de Sousa Amado, entitled *Documents et Reflexions*, in which he stated that three or four Freemasons had been appointed to bishoprics. One of these, he said, was Dr. Joseph Marie da Silva Torre, Archbishop of Goa, who had been initiated in the Lodge Urbionia de Coimbra. The author also complained that it was the government's intention to present to the Holy See the names of two well-known Freemasons for consecration to the episcopacy, these being L'Abbe Emmanuel Cardoso Napoles and Dr. Antoine Aires de Gouveia.

In 1873 the Jesuits, driven from most of the European countries, selected Brazil as a field for their enterprise. For a long time the Church and Freemasons had lived in peace, and the population of Pernambuco had always been recognized as a type of Christian piety. But the Bishop of the diocese, a young man of only twenty-three years of age, at the bidding of the Jesuits, attempted to enforce the Papal Bull against the Freemasons. The prelate had counted on the support of the people, but his high-handed measures turned the tide of popular feeling. The Bishop was mobbed in his own palace, and the military had to be called in to protect him.

In January, 1874, the Roman Catholic Archbishop of Molines, Primate of Belgium, issued a pastoral in which he excommunicated all Freemasons in the kingdom, however exalted their position. This, notwithstanding the fact that the Constitution of Belgium guarantees freedom of conscience to all religious communities so long as they do not violate the law of the State.

In the same month, says the *Valparaiso Mail*, quoting from the *Opinion Nacionale* of Rosario, "the Bishop of Rio Grande excommunicated and anathematized the Freemasons of that province, cursing them in the name of God the Father, God the Son, and God the Holy Ghost, of St. Peter, St. Paul, and St. Andrew, of all the Apostles and disciples of Jesus Christ, of the four Evangelists, of all the Martyrs from the beginning of the world to the end of time. He cursed them all by the heavens and the earth, all the things therein, in their houses, when travelling on land and on water, in church, coming, going, eating, drinking, playing, when courting sleep, asleep and awake, walking, riding, sitting, working, and resting. He cursed all the power of their bodies, interior and exterior, their hair, eyes, head, ears, jaws, nose, teeth, throat, shoulders, arms, legs, feet, all the joints, and finally wound up as follows: 'Curse them, Jesus Christ, Son of the Living God, with all the power of Thy majesty, and may they be delivered up to eternal condemnation if they do not repent and confess their faults. Amen. Amen."'

In May, 1875, Pope Pius IX sent the following letter to Monsignor Dupanloup:

"Venerable Brother:- Salutation and Apostolical Benediction. In this war waged on all sides against the Catholic Church by the Masonic sect, your publication was most useful and opportune, especially because this sect, long secret, has now unmasked itself. It avows its designs, and in a certain country, not under the pretext of public rights, but in its own name, does guilty battle with the Church. It is useful, because the nefarious character of the sect being known, there is no honest man who must not turn from it with horror, and perhaps many members who do not know the secret mysteries will now withdraw. What is particularly useful is the perspicacity with which you demonstrate to all attentive minds the real tendency of the taking words 'Fraternity and Equality,' which have deceived and seduced so many, and the true origin and object of the much boasted liberties of conscience, of public worship, and of the press. After reading your work nobody can doubt that all this came from Freemasonry to overturn civil and religious order, and consequently the Church has wisely condemned those who practice and defend such liberties. It is manifest that all partisans of these liberties, albeit unknown to themselves, favor the Masonic sect, and the more honest they are, the more disastrous is their support to such principles. We therefore wish you many intelligent readers, for it is no small advantage to perceive the snare, and as a pledge of Divine favor and our special goodwill we give you, Venerable Brother, from the bottom of our heart, to you and your diocese, our Apostolical Benediction. In the twenty-third year of our Pontificate. Pius IX, Pope."

In 1877, on the occasion of the anniversary of the consecration of Pope Pius IX as Archbishop of Spoleto, the Catholics of Portugal, particularly the Michaelists, to which Order reference has been made in these columns, falling in with the practice being adopted by other countries, organized a pilgrimage to Rome. About three hundred Portuguese joined in the excursion. They were received at Rome, when, in response to an address presented to him, Pope Pius IX said, among other things: "You have a powerful and terrible enemy, that is violent Freemasonry, which wishes to annihilate in you all vestiges of Catholicism."

In 1878 Monsignor Besson, Bishop of Nismes, issued an edict forbidding the intrusion of Masonic emblems into the churches of his diocese and ordering the priests to remove them whenever found.

On 20th April, 1884, Pope Leo XIII issued his famous Letter *Humanum Genus* "To all venerable Patriarchs, Primates, Archbishops, and Bishops in the Catholic world who have grace and communion with the Apostolic See." (See: Appendix along with the answer by Albert Pike)

The Bishop of Ascalon, Vicar-Apostolic of Bombay, in a pastoral letter promulgating the Encyclical Letter, said:

"In the performance of their duty the parish priests and confessors must not admit as valid or reasonable the common excuse that Freemasonry, in India and England aims at nothing but social amusement, mutual advancement, and charitable benevolence. Such objects require neither a terrible oath of secrecy nor an elaborate system and scale of numerous degrees, nor a connection with the Masonic lodges of other countries, about whose anti-Christian, anti-social, and revolutionary character and aim no doubt nor further concealment is possible. The Masonic lodges all over the world are firmly knitted and bound together in solidarity. If all of them share in the pleasure of a triumph achieved by a particular lodge, or by the lodges of a particular country, all must likewise submit to the stigma of an anti-Christian, anti-social, and revolutionary sect, as which Freemasonry is in many countries already openly known, and even unblushingly confessed by its own adepts."

It goes without saying that the Jesuits proclaimed against "Freemasonry the same anathemas as the heads of the Roman Church, and this is demonstrated by the following circular letter signed by Vincent Ficarelli, Provincial of the Jesuits in Portugal, which was sent in 1884 to all the houses of that Society in that country:

"Reverend Fathers and very dear Brethren: The Peace of Christ be with you. The Very Reverend Father Vicar-General, hastening to the appeal made by the Holy Father to all Catholics to combat secret societies has addressed to all the Society an Encyclical Letter, in which he invites all his children to take part in this glorious campaign.

"Indeed, says the Reverend Father Vicar, it is not sufficient to read but once that admirable *Encyclical Humanum Genus*, but it is necessary that it be meditated upon with attention in order firmly to impress upon the mind what is contained in the same and this, up to a certain point, is what concerns this letter. That also is why I wish all those to whom this has reference, shall not remain content with hearing it read in the refectory, but that they shall consider it attentively and strive well to make it take a firm grip of their minds.

"It is a question of combatting the most terrible enemy of the Church, which boasting in the victories obtained up to the present, believes itself to be altogether the conqueror, and proclaims that nothing further can come into opposition with its dark designs. To us, as obedient children, it should suffice to enlist courageously in the fight, knowing what is the will of the Vicar of Jesus Christ, whom Divine Providence has given to us as father, mother, and guide of our actions. Having therefore courage, and with the cry 'God wills it' let us hasten to enlist in this glorious crusade.

'It is a question of agreement with the Sovereign Pontiff and all good men will attend to us. Let all, in obedience to the voice of Leo XIII, take up arms against the common enemy. Let not the difficulties discourage us: such do not lessen the zeal of our enemies. Let us count on the blessing of God and go forward.

"We must all contribute to the success of the enterprise. Let confessors and spiritual directors, particularly of young men, by their counsels and opportune remonstrances, endeavour to form the minds of their penitents and pupils by insinuating the principles of the Faith and of the Christian philosophy, by opposing the doctrine of naturalism professed by this abominable sect. Let preachers and writers profit by every prudent opportunity by attacking directly or indirectly the secret societies and combatting their doctrines. Guided always by obedience and prudence, let none lose a single opportunity of causing hatred to Freemasonry, in conversations and in private letters, in religious instructions and sermons, in the exercises of the clergy and others of the faithful, in missions and particularly in colleges, let us seek seriously to counteract its deleterious action.

"Let us exert ourselves to warn our pupils against the maneuvers of Freemasonry, making them to see its abominable character, in order that they may detest it as much as it deserves. Let us have a particular care of Confraternities, particularly those composed of men and attached to our Society, by opposing those diabolical societies and contrasting them with our own, where the Gospel maxims are inculcated unceasingly, and thus we shall introduce, or rather, engrave by degrees in the hearts of our members the mind of Jesus Christ and the love of the Christian virtues.

"It is for the Superiors to direct these movements, that the excessive zeal of the indiscreet may be put down and the valor of the more indolent stimulated, in order that prudence may not be relaxed nor courage reach to indiscretion and temerity.

"I desire that this letter in which I have sought to do my utmost to assemble the principal ideas of the Encyclical Letter of our Reverend Father Vicar-General, should come to the knowledge of all, and in order that it may produce the good which I desire let us invoke the wisdom and the grace of the Holy Spirit.

"I commend myself to your prayers.

"Lisbon, 15th July, 1884.

(Father) "Vincent Ficarelli, S. J."

In accordance with the commands of the Provincial, the Jesuits compelled their followers before entering the Congregation of the Holy Virgin to make the following declaration:

"Obeying with a filial love the authority of the Vicar of Jesus Christ, clearly expressed in the *Encyclical Humanum Genus* by His Holiness, Leo XIII, who, as well as the Sovereign Pontiffs, his predecessors, has frequently condemned Freemasonry and all other secret societies, I undertake and promise never to enrol myself in any one of these sects, no matter by what name it may be called. On the contrary, I will valiantly combat, always and everywhere, its traditions, doctrines, and influence. So help me God."

This oath, it must be remembered, was frequently taken by young children.

An Encyclical Letter to the Bishops of Italy, entitled *Ab Apostolici* was issued by Pope Leo XIII on 15th October, 1890, in which he said:

"It is needless now to put the Masonic sects upon their trial. They are already judged, their ends, their means, their doctrines, and their action are all known with indisputable certainty. Possessed by the spirit of Satan, whose instrument they are, they burn, like him, with a deadly and implacable hatred of Jesus Christ and of His work; and they endeavour by every means to overthrow and fetter it: . . . It is more than ever clear that the ruling idea which, as far as religion is concerned, controls the course of public affairs in Italy, is the realization of the Masonic program. We see how much has already been realized; we know how much still remains to be done; and we can foresee with certainty that, so long as the destinies of Italy are in the hands of sectarian rulers or of men subject to the sects, the realization of the program will be pressed on, more or less rapidly according to circumstances, unto its complete development. The action of the sects is at present directed to attain the following objects, according to the votes and resolutions passed in their most important assemblies, votes and resolutions inspired throughout by a deadly hatred of the Church: (1) the abolition in the schools of every kind of religious instruction, and the founding of institutions in which even girls are to be withdrawn from all clerical influence whatever it may be; because the State, which ought to be absolutely atheistic, has the inalienable right and duty to form the heart and the spirit of its citizens, and no school should exist apart from its inspiration and control. The rigorous application of all laws now in force, which aim at securing the absolute independence of civil society from clerical influence. The strict observance of laws suppressing religious corporations, and the employment of means to make them effectual. The regulations, of all ecclesiastical property, starting from the principle that its ownership belongs to the State, and its administration to the civil power. The exclusion of every Catholic or clerical element from all public administrations, from pious works, hospitals and schools, from the councils which govern the doctrines of the country, from academical and other unions, from companies, committees, and families, the exclusion from everything, everywhere, and for ever. Instead, the Masonic influence is to make itself felt in all the circumstances of social life and to become master and controller of everything. Hereby the way will be smoothed towards the abolition of the Papacy; Italy will thus be free from its implacable and deadly enemy; and Rome which, in the past, was the centre of universal theocracy, will, in the future, be the centre of universal secularization, once the mocking charity of human liberty is to be proclaimed in the face of the world. Such are the atheistic declarations, aspirations, and resolutions of Freemasons or of their assemblies."

On Christmas Day, 1891, Pope Leo XIII issued another Encyclical Letter, one clause of which ran as follows:

"Permit us, then, in addressing you, to point to Masonry as the enemy at once of God, the Church, and our country. Since we are dealing with a sect which has spread itself everywhere, it is not enough to be on the defensive towards it, but we must go courageously into the arena and meet it, as you will do, dear children, by opposing press to press, school to school, association to association, congress to congress, action to action."

The late Cardinal Vaughan was one of the most affable of men, who seldom - in contrast with other members of his family - entered the public arena of verbal conflict and discussion. His knowledge of Freemasonry must have been extremely limited, even for one outside the Order, to imagine that the Third Order of St. Francis, admirable organization though it may be, could ever rise to the equal of the Craft of Freemasonry. But, on one occasion, the Cardinal wrote in one of his pastoral letters:

"Who, when he beholds the enemies of Christianity leaguing together in a world-wide Freemasonry, in order to attain by combination that which they feel they could never otherwise achieve - who will not at once admit the wisdom of founding the Third Order of St. Francis, which binds devout Christians together in every part of the world in a holy confederacy, having for its sole object the service of God and the conversation and reformation of society."

An ancient saying is that often-misquoted - *De mortuis nil nisi bonum* - but it is a remarkable fact that when attacking a system or creed the opponents will, not infrequently, commit themselves to the most outrageous statements and still persevere in them, even when their falsity has been proved most conclusively. This is particularly the case with Protestant critics of the Roman system. Certainly this feature is not met with so frequently among Catholic apologists, but that it is not unknown may be proved from the statement in the next paragraph.

Lecturing at the Hempstead Town Hall in March, 1898, the late Dr. Luke Rivington said that any one acquainted with the history of Italy achieving her unity could only blush if he had a spark of Christian feeling in him. It was only during the last few years since we had seen the letters of Garibaldi that we had become aware of the iniquity, the disgrace, and the positive barbarism of all that matter, and of the awful disgraceful lies told by the Freemasons of Italy. Christians must blush to think that anyone bearing the name of Christian should enter upon a course of such disgraceful meanness and shocking falsehood. There was no nation under heaven at that moment so trodden down by oppression and tyranny as the Italian poor. As one who, had mixed among them he knew how heavily they were taxed. It was something too dreadful to think about, and he looked upon the matter as a blot upon our civilization. As one who had been a Freemason, he could say that most of them believed, and he among the number, that once when Crispi was admitted to a certain degree, he began to worship the devil himself. The whole state of Italy was something so perfectly awful that most people felt they were on the verge of a revolution. They had succeeded in introducing secular education for a whole generation, and they had no right to speak of a nation as being in the undisputed possession of the Roman Catholic Church when, as a matter of fact, Freemasonry had got into that country. Freemasonry was a secret society which walked in darkness, and had put in its program secular education in order to destroy religion. . . . So far as history went when the Roman Catholic Church had perfect possession of a nation, then that nation rose to the top. That was the case with Spain. It was the leading power of Europe. The Freemasons had not got there then, and so long as the Roman Catholic Church had possession of a nation, so long it would find its way upwards and upwards. Dismiss the Freemasons and bring back the Pope and they would have the best governor in the whole of Europe.

The foregoing is taken from a Roman Catholic newspaper report of the lecture, published in the following week, but the outrageous statements made therein do not appear to have been brought to the notice of the Masonic press at that date. Otherwise it is certain that a challenge would have been issued to Dr Luke Rivington, member of the Craft of Freemasonry though he may have been at an earlier date, to have proved the statements made. At any rate the opposing statement may, here be made in issue - that in no degree in Freemasonry recognized by the United Grand Lodge of England or in any of the Jurisdictions with which she is in communion will there be found anything approaching to the worship of the devil, nor is there single degree into which any one can be admitted and remain a member who does not acknowledge and maintain, without equivocation, his sole dependence upon that One Great, Supreme Power - God, the Almighty Creator and Preserver of Mankind.

Yet another Pastoral Letter, entitled *Annum in gressi* was issued by Pope Leo XIII, on 18th March, 1902, which may be regarded as complimentary to Freemasonry, inasmuch as if the Craft had not mad rapid and increasing strides, there would not have been the need for these frequent diatribes. Referring to the charges of political ambition brought against the Church in France and Italy, the Pope said:

"It is then, assuredly, with a perverse intention that accusations such as these are hurled against the Church. A pernicious and disloyal task this, in the pursuit of which the leading part is taken by a certain secret sect, which, for many years past, society has carried in its alliance, and which, like the germ of mortal disease, saps its health, its fruitfulness, its very life. A enduring personification of revolutionary principles, it constitutes a kind of perverted society, whose object is to exercise a hidden suzerainty over recognized society, and the very reason of whose being is nothing else than to wage war against God and against his Church. It is needless to name it, for by these characteristics ever one must have recognized that we mean Freemasonry of which we spoke in express terms in our *Encyclical Humanuin Genus* of the 20th April, 1894, wherein we denounced its destructive tendencies, its erroneous doctrines, its wicked work. Embracing, as it does, in it vast net almost all the nations, and allying itself with other sects which it sets in motion by means of hidden springs first attaching and then keeping its hold on its members by means of the advantages which it secures to them, binding governments to its purposes, now by promises, now by threats, this sect has succeeded in permeating all classes of society. It forms a kind of invisible and irresponsible state within the legitimate State. Filled with the spirit of Satan, who, as the Apostle tells us, knows how, on occasion, to transform himself into an angel of light (II Cor. xi, 14) it puts prominently forward a humanitarian program, but, in fact, it sacrifices everything to its sectarian designs. It pretends that it has no political aim, but, in truth, it exercises a profound influence over the legislative and administrative life of states. And, whereas, in words it professes respect for authority and even for religion, its ultimate purpose (as appears from its own constitutions) is a limitation of the sovereign power and of the priesthood, in which it professes to see enemies of liberty.

"Now, it becomes daily more manifest that to the instigation and active consultants of this sect must, in great measure, be ascribed the continual vexations wherewith the Church is harassed and the renewed attacks which have, quite recently, been made upon her. For the simultaneousness of the assaults which have been delivered, the suddenness of the persecution which has broken out in these last days, like a storm in a clear sky, that is to say without any cause proportioned to the effect produced; the uniformity of the preparations carried out by means of attacks in the press, in public meetings, and in theatrical representations; the employment in every country of the same arms, namely, calumnies aid popular risings - all these unmistakably betoken an identity of purpose and a word of command which is issued from one only centre of direction. This, indeed, is a mere episode in a preconcerted plan of campaign, which is translating itself into action on a stage that grows ever wider and wider, in order to multiply the ruinous consequences which we have heretofore enumerated. Its very purpose is first to restrict and afterwards entirely to abolish religious education, and thereby to bring up generations of unbelievers or indifferentists; to combat, by means of the daily press, the morality of the Church; to ridicule her practices and to prevent her sacred festivals.

"Nothing is more natural, then, that the Catholic priesthood, whose mission is no other than that of preaching religion and administering the sacraments, should be attacked with special fury. Having chosen the priesthood as an object to be aimed at, this sect seeks to diminish in the eyes of the people its prestige and authority. Already, with a boldness which increases hourly and in proportion to the impunity which it believes itself to have secured, it puts a malign interpretation on all the acts of the clergy; it mistrusts them on the, slightest pretext, and harasses them with the basest charges. And these fresh injuries are added to those under which the clergy already suffer, in spite of the tribute which it must pay to military service, a serious obstacle to the preparation of its members for the priesthood, as well as the consequence of the confiscation of the patrimony of the Church, which the faithful, out of their pious generosity, had voluntarily created."

In October, 1913, Pope Pius X recommended to the League of the Sacred Heart, as the intention of the members for the month, the battle against Freemasonry. A Roman Catholic newspaper announcing the fact, said:

"In offering to the associates of the League of the Sacred Heart, and thereby to the entire Catholic world, the battle against Freemasonry as the primal intention of their prayers and practices for October, Pope Pius X is in unison with all his predecessors from Clement XII in 1738, to Pope Leo XIII in 1890, who condemned Freemasonry as anti-Catholic, anti-Christian and immoral, and pronounced excommunication against Catholics who should enter it.

"This alone is proof sufficient that Masonry is to be avoided and combatted as a thing essentially evil; yet it has cunningly persuaded many that its object is merely social and fraternal, and a large number of 'outer' Masons in English-speaking countries are kept ignorant of its real designs."

In 1916, in the course of an address at the fourth annual meeting of the Australian Catholic Federation at Melbourne, Archbishop Mannix said:

"I wish that the Federation could boast in its report that it had at some point met, unmasked, and overthrown the most insidious enemy of God and country, the Freemason Brotherhood. Catholics who know Australian life better than I can pretend to know it, assure me that the sinister influence of that body is felt at every turn - in polities, in trade, in commerce, in the professions. From the making of a law and the shaping of a policy to the letting of a contract and the hiring of a wharf laborer, the secret grip of the brotherhood makes itself felt, and not for the common good, but for the exclusive good of the Freemasons. Already in this young democratic country we have, apparently, this secret aristocracy fastened upon the neck of Australia, a huge tumour, feeding upon the very vitals, the blood, and the life of the country. The Prime Minister recently used strong language about those whom he described as parasites upon the Labor Party. He is a strong man and a man of courage. I wish that he felt himself free enough and strong enough to deal with those that are not parasites upon any one party, but who are poisoning the public life of all parties, who are strangling honesty in commerce, and who are battening not on a party, but on the Australian nation. If the Federation could only unmask some of the brethren it would be helping to purify Australian life. Perhaps, for a small beginning, the Federation might make a list of the Freemasons who sit as Federal or State members. The list should have great interest for all democratic Australians at election times. For I have no doubt that the secret understandings among the Masonic brethren would explain much that is done behind the backs and against the will of the people."

This statement is quoted only as a sample of the many utterances of Catholic priests and prelates, who certainly cannot know what they are talking about. Certainly no credence need be placed in this particular utterance when the career of Archbishop Mannix is considered, along with his treasonable utterances and his lack of respect for anything that would "purify" life.

CHAPTER VIII

THE STATEMENT is made very frequently both in the Roman Catholic press and from the pulpit that members of that faith are not permitted by their church or papal decree to become members of any secret society whatever may be their constitution or however harmless their character. In accordance with such interpretation of Roman Catholic jurisprudence, consistent Catholics refrain from associating themselves with the Masonic Order, and also from such organizations as Druidism, Forestry, Buffaloism, Ancient Britons, and the like. The Roman Catholic statement, however, demands qualification, for the prohibition applies only to societies not under the jurisdiction or government or oversight of the Roman Catholic clergy. For there are affiliated to the Church in all parts of the world certain societies to which only Roman Catholics may belong, which have certain forms of initiation or admission, which meet behind closed doors, their minutes of proceedings not being published; some of which, moreover, engage in revolutionary propaganda, which constitutional acts are inhibited by Masonic Constitutions.

One of the most famous and active of these societies at the present day is that known as the Knights of Columbus, which, as a body, has recently recognized officially the existence of an Irish republic, with Eamon de Valera as its president, and which has passed resolutions urging the United States Senate and House of Representatives to do the same without delay. The object underlying such resolution is apparent. It is well recognized that were the Senate and House of Representatives to do any such thing, there would, at once, be an open break in the diplomatic relations between the United Kingdom and the United States, which might, and not improbably, result in another outbreak of war. The Knights of Columbus, which is a very powerful organization, limited in membership to Roman Catholics, has been, not inaptly, described as the Pope's most powerful secret society in America; yet we do not read that this resolution has received papal condemnation or disapproval, so that it may quite fairly be assumed that it has the papal sanction. There is ample proof in many published statements that the members of this society work under clerical direction: the following quotation will suffice. In 1916, Archbishop Munderlin, in an address to the Knights of Columbus, as reported in the *Chicago Evening American* of 9th March, 1916, said: "I will expect you to be ready. I am your leader, your thinker, and your director. I will tell you what to do and will expect you to do it. I need you men. Never differ from your bishop. He thinks for you."

There is in Ireland, America, and other counties, another society of a similar character. It is known as the *Order of Hibernians*, and it is a continuation of the famous Ribbon Society, which was prominent in Irish life some years ago. These Ribbonmen appeared in the early part of the nineteenth century, after the suppression of the rebellion in 1798, and was formed from among the surviving members of the United Irishmen, Whiteboys and Defenders, all of whom took an oath "to burn, destroy, and murder all heretics up to my knees in blood." Each Ribbonman took an oath (see *Report of Select Committee on the State of Ireland*, 1832) in the following words: "I swear I will to the best of my power cut down kings, queens, and princes, dukes, lords, earls, and all such, with land-jobbing and heresy. I swear I will never pity the moans and groans of the dying from the cradle to the crutch, and that I will wade knee deep in Orange blood." All these societies were under the direction and control of the Catholic clergy, confined in their membership to Roman Catholics, and among their objects were to assist Roman Catholicism and the visionary idea of Ireland as an independent nation. The system did not receive the support of all Irish Catholics. Mr. A. M. Sullivan, his work, New Ireland, (seventh edition, pp. 41 and 42) says:

"But alas! when one comes to review the actual results of the Ribbon system in Ireland - to survey its bloody work throughout those fifty years - how frightful is the prospect? It has been said, and probably with some truth, that it has been too much the habit to attribute erroneously to the Ribbon organization every atrocity committed in the country, every deed of blood arising out of agrarian combination or conspiracy. An emphatic denial, and challenge to proofs, have been given to stories of midnight trials and sentences of death at lodge meetings. Very possibly the records of lodge meetings afford no such proof, though there is abundant evidence that at such assemblages threatening notices and warnings were ordered to be served and domiciliary visits for terrorizing purposes were decreed. But vain is all pretence that the Ribbon Society did not become, whatever the original design and intention of its members may have been, a hideous organization of outrage and murder. It is one of the inherent evils of oath-bound secret societies of this kind, where implicit obedience to secret superiors is sworn, that they may very easily and quickly drop to the lowest level of demoralization, and become associations for the wreaking of mere personal vengeance."

In the concluding paragraph of the chapter devoted by Mr. A.M. Sullivan to "The Ribbon Conspiracy' (it must be remembered that Mr. Sullivan was a Roman Catholic and a Nationalist), he says:

"From 1835 to 1855 the Ribbon organization was at its greatest strength. For the last fifteen or twenty years" (he wrote in 1877) "it has been gradually disappearing from the greater part of Ireland, yet, strange to say, betimes intensifying, in a baser and more malignant form than ever, in one or two localities. With the emigration of the laboring classes it was carried abroad, to England and to America. At one time the most formidable lodges were in Lancashire, whether, it is said, the headquarters were removed for safety."

In America the society became known under various names, such as the "Molly Maguires," "Buckshots," etc., and there are some interesting details concerning its machinations and iniquities to be read in E. W. Lucy's book, *The Moly Maguires*, particularly the sworn evidences of Detective McParlan. Membership was confined to Roman Catholics of Irish birth or parentage. At the time in its history of which Lucy wrote, it had an elaborate organization, each lodge consisting of a president or body-master, together with a vice body-master, secretary, assistant secretary, and treasurer, making five officers at the head of each lodge. Then there were higher bodies, which had each a county delegate, county secretary, and county treasurer, who were assisted by a county committee. Above these were state officers, consisting of state delegate, state secretary, and state treasurer; while, above these again, were national organizations, consisting each of national delegate, national secretary, national treasurer, and president of the Board. But the over-ruling body was known as the Board of Erin, which consisted of representatives from England, Ireland, and Scotland, which met at various intervals, in one or other of the three countries. The members of the main body were known to each other by signs and pass-words, or sentences, which were issued by the Board of Erin and changed four times in the year. Some of these are given in Lucy's book. One ran:

"The Emperor of France and Don Carlos of Spain, They unite together and the Pope's right maintain; the response being:

"Will tenant right in Ireland flourish, If the people unite and the landlords subdue?"

Another ran:

"That the trouble of the country may soon be at an end, to which the answer was given:

"And likewise the man who will not her defend.

"Later, in Beaconsfield's time, the greeting between members was:

"What do you think of Disraeli's plan, Who still keeps Home Rule from our native land?

"The answer to which was:

"But still with good words and men at command We will give long-lost rights to our native land.

"During part of 1875 the greeting was changed to:

"Gladstone's policy must be put down, He is the main support of the British crown; to which the fellow-member made reply:

"But our Catholic lords will not support his plan, For true to their Church they will firmly stand."

William Carleton, in his interesting novel, *The Tithe Procter*, a novel, be it remembered, founded absolutely on fact, proof of which is given by him in the preface, and a novel which deals entirely with the machinations of a secret society, the membership of which was limited to Roman Catholics, says:

"The condition of all secret and illegal societies in Ireland is, indeed, shocking and most detestable, when contemplated from any point of view whatsoever. In every one of them - that is, in every local, body, or branch of that conspiracy - there is a darker and more secret class, comparatively few in number, who undertake to organize the commission of crimes and out-rages; and who, in cases where they are controlled by the peaceably-disposed and enemies to bloodshed, always fall back upon this private and blood-stained clique, who are always willing to execute their sanguinary behests, as it were, *con amore*. In other cases, however, as we have stated before, even the virtuous and reluctant are often compelled, by the dark and stem decrees of these desperate ruffians, to perpetrate crimes from which they revolt."

The most important secret society, from the Roman Catholic point of view, is that great and wonderful organization, the Society of Jesus, better known, perhaps, as the Jesuits. It consists, not only of the clergy, and of these there are two classes, professed and unprofessed, but also of various branches of lay associations and societies. There are also various sodalities, meeting ostensibly for devotional practices and religious purposes, but which meet in secret conclave, initiated members only being admitted. The most important of these latter is that known as the *Prima Premaria*. This society was founded in 1563, and established canonically in 1584, by a Bull issued by Gregory XIII, and which was attached to it a number of branches in all parts of the world. The suppression of the Society of Jesus in 1773, says Waterton, in *Pietas Mariana Britannica*, "did not affect the Prima Premaria, for the ex-members who continued under the name of the English Academy, kept up the sodality until they were driven out of Liege in 1794, in which year they came to England and established themselves at Stonyhurst. Consequently, the Stonyhurst sodality, tracing an unbroken descent from the year 1617, is, perhaps, the oldest existing branch in the world of the Prima Primaria." In December, 1857, a branch was founded at the well-known London Jesuit church in Farm Street, Berkeley Square, W, "for gentlemen only." One of its rules is that "only those are to be admitted into the congregation who are in a respectable position in life and with some pretensions to a literary education." Another runs: "Upon sodalists, moreover, it is enjoined that they should always obey, with a prompt and ready will, the counsels and commands of their directors." Yet another says: "The immediate superior of the congregation of the Prima Primaria, by virtue of the Apostolic Constitution, is the Father General of the Society of Jesus. To him consequently belongs the government of the Congregation: it is in his power to make laws; revoke or modify them, since everything depends on his authority." Another rule given in the Manual for the use of Sodalities affiliated to the Prima Primaria tells us that "those are excluded from the congregation who suffer from epileptic fits, or are physically or accidentally deformed."

Another society, also closely connected with the Jesuits, is that known as the "Holy League of the Heart of Jesus," all members of which have to make the following solemn promise: "Freemasonry and all other secret societies having been condemned by the infallible voice and authority of the Vicar of Christ. I . . . . obedient to that authority, solemnly resolve and engage never to belong to any such secret association, under whatever name it may be called; but, on the contrary, to oppose to the utmost of my power, their influence, their teaching, and their acts. Amen."

This obligation is elaborated in the *Handbook of the League*, where part of the constitutions is set out as follows:

"Our reverend directors, our promoters and associates, will understand the motives which should prompt the Director General of the Holy League to issue the following instructions: In order the more thoroughly to enter into the intention of the Holy Father expressed in the teaching of the late Encyclical Letter, *Humanum Genus*, (directed against Freemasonry), we earnestly beg of all our Directors, both diocesan and local, to require in all receptions of associates of either sex to the Holy League, and, in the case of our promoters, as a necessary condition, the promise never to enter into any secret society, and not to give encouragement or help to any of them."

It may not, perhaps, be known generally that some of the branches of the Children of Mary, the members of which form an attractive and striking figure in many open-air Roman Catholic processions, now so frequent in the summer months, are branches of the Prima Primaria, erected by a diploma of the General of the Society of Jesus, and enjoy all privileges of indulgence attached to it in common with all other sodalists. A distinction, says Waterton, must, therefore, be made between the Children of Mary, or lady sodalists, who are affiliated to the Prima Primaxia, and those local or conventual fraternities, known by the same name.

In 1877, Pope Pius IX organized the "Militia of Jesus Christ," a Catholic Crusaders association, which had as its third aim: "to array against the powerful organization of the secret societies leagued against the Lord, and His own innumerable army of devoted Catholics, ready to fight in open day, with all the means at its power, those who work in secret and in darkness." It is unnecessary to point out that the objects of the attack were not the Jesuits and other Roman Catholic secret societies, who, undoubtedly, correspond thoroughly to the description given. According to a correspondent of the Daily News this Militia numbered more than a million members, principally in France and Belgium, within a very short time of its formation.

In the *Memoirs of Saint-Simon* (Volume III, p. 268, 1902 ed.), we are told that "the Jesuits constantly admit the laity, even married, into their company. The fact is certain. There is no doubt that Des Noyers, secretary of state under Louis XIII, was of this number, and that many others have been so too. These licentiates make the same vow as the Jesuits, so far as their condition admits: that is, unrestricted obedience to the General, and to the superiors of the Company. They are obliged to comply with the vows of poverty and chastity by promising to give all the service and all the protection in their power to the Company; above all, to be entirely submissive to the superiors and to their confessor. They are obliged to perform with exactitude such light exercises of piety as their confessor may have adapted to the circumstances of their lives, and that he simplifies as much as he likes. It answers the purposes of the Company to ensure to itself those hidden auxiliaries. But nothing must pass through their minds, nothing must come to their knowledge that they do not reveal to their confessor, and to the superiors, if the confessor thinks fit. In everything, too, they must obey, without comment the superior and the confessor." This, of course, is in accordance with the enormous claims made by the Church of Rome, not only to be the administrator of the laws of God, but also to be empowered to make fresh laws, which must be obeyed with equal rigidity, under penalties and punishments. This claim is well set forth by the Rev. Edmund J. O'Reilly, S. J., in his book, The Relations of the Church to Society, wherein he says: "The Church's jurisdiction, like that of any State, comprises legislative an executive powers. The Church not only administers divine laws, but makes laws herself. Some of them are in great measure identified with her administrate of divine law. She imposes on her subjects the obligation of receiving her declarations of faith, and, more less, under ecclesiastical penalties. But, besides doing this, she imposes other obligations in connection with faith and morals. She commands and forbids acts that are not already respectively commanded or forbidden by God. All this she does for the better attainment of her end, which is the salvation of souls. These laws of the Church are human laws, enacted in virtue of authority received from God, but still human laws, liable to abrogation, mortification, and dispensation, where circumstances may so require or render expedient."

APPENDIX

THE ENCYCLICAL LETTER "HUMANUM GENUS"
OF THE POPE LEO XIII

April 20th, 1884

To all venerable Patriarchs, Primates, Archbishops, and Bishops in the Catholic world who have grace and communion with the Apostolic See: Venerable Brothers: Health and the Apostolic Benedictions

THE HUMAN RACE, after, by the malice of the devil, it had departed from God, the Creator and Giver of heavenly gifts, divided itself into two different and opposing parties, one of which assiduously combats for truth and virtue, the other for those things which are opposed to virtue and to truth. The one is the Kingdom of God on earth that is, the Church of Jesus Christ; those who desire to adhere to which from their soul and conductively to salvation must serve God and His only begotten Son with their whole mind and their whole will. The other is the kingdom of Satan, in whose dominion and power are all who have followed his sad example and that of our first parents. They refuse to obey divine and eternal law, and strive for many things to the neglect of God and for many against God. This twofold kingdom, like two states with contrary laws working in contrary directions, Augustine clearly saw and described, and comprehended the efficient cause of both with subtle brevity in these words: "Two loves have made two states: the love of self to the contempt of God has made the earthly, but the love of God to the contempt of self has made the heavenly." (De Civ. Dei, lib. xiv., chap. 17.)

The one fights the other with different kinds of weapons, and battles at all times, though not always with the same ardor and fury. In our days, however, those who follow the evil one seem to conspire and strive all together under the guidance and with the help of that society of men spread all over, and solidly established, which they call Free-Masons. Not dissimulating their intentions, they vie in attacking the power of God; they openly and ostensibly strive to damage the Church, with the purpose to deprive thoroughly if possible Christian people of the benefits brought by the Savior Jesus Christ.

Seeing these evils, we are compelled by charity in our soul to say often to God: "For lo! Thy enemies have made noise; and they that hate Thee have lifted up the head. They have taken malicious counsel against Thy people, and have consulted against Thy saints. They have said: Come and let us destroy them, so that they be not a nation." (Ps. lxxxii., 24.)

In such an impending crisis, in such a great and obstinate warfare upon

Christianity, it is our duty to point out the danger, exhibit the adversaries, resist as much as we can their schemes and tricks, lest those whose salvation is in our hands should perish eternally: and that the kingdom of Jesus Christ, which we have received in trust, not only may stay and remain intact, but may continue to increase all over the world by new additions.

The Roman Pontiffs, our predecessors, watching constantly over the safety of the Christian people, early recognized this capital enemy rushing forth out of the darkness of hidden conspiracy, and, anticipating the future in their mind, gave the alarm to princes and people, that they should not be caught by deceptions and frauds.

Clement XII first signalized the danger in 1738, and Benedict XIV renewed and continued his Constitution. Pius VII followed them both; and Leo XII, by the Apostolic Constitution *quo graviora* recapitulating the acts and decrees of the above Pontiffs about the manner, validated and confirmed them forever. In the same way spoke Pius VIII, Gregory XVI, and very often Pius IX.

The purpose and aim of the Masonic sect having been discovered from plain evidence, from the cognition of causes, its laws, Rites and commentaries having come to light and been made known by the additional depositions of the associated members, this Apostolic See denounced and openly declared that the sect of Masons is established against law and honesty, and is equally a danger to Christianity as well as to society; and, threatening those heavy punishments which the Church uses against the guilty ones, she forbade the society, and ordered that none should give his name to it. Therefore the angry Masons, thinking that they would escape the sentence or partially destroy it by despising or calumniating, accused the Pope who made those decrees of not having made a right decree or of having overstepped moderation. They thus tried to evade the authority and the importance of the Apostolic Constitutions of Clement XII, Benedict XIV, Pius VII, and Pius IX. But in the same society there were some who, even against their own will, acknowledged that the Roman Pontiffs had acted wisely and lawfully, according to the Catholic discipline. In this many princes and rulers of States agreed with the Popes, and either denounced Masonry to the Apostolic See or by appropriate laws condemned it as a bad thing in Holland, Austria, Switzerland, Spain, Bavaria, Savoy, and other parts of Italy.

But the event justified the prudence of our predecessors, and this is the most important. Nay, their paternal care did not always and everywhere succeed, either because of the simulation and shrewdness of the Masons themselves, or through the inconsiderate levity of others whose duty required of them strict attention. Hence, in a century and a half the sect of Masons grew beyond expectation; and, creeping audaciously and deceitfully among the various classes of the people, it grew to be so powerful that now it seems the only dominating power in the States. From this rapid and dangerous growth have come into the Church and into the State those evils which our predecessors had already foreseen. It has indeed come to this, that we have serious fear, not for the Church, which has a foundation too firm for men to upset it, but for those States in which this society is so powerful or other societies of a like kind, and which show themselves to be servants and companions of Masonry.

For these reasons, when we first succeeded in the government of the Church, we saw and felt very clearly the necessity of opposing so great an evil with the full weight of our authority. On all favorable occasions we have attacked the principal doctrines in which the Masonic perversity appeared. By our Encyclical Letter, *quod apostolic muneris*, we attacked the errors of Socialists and Communists; by the Letter, *Arcanum*, we tried to explain and defend the genuine notion of domestic society, whose source and origin is in marriage; finally, by the letter which begins Diuturnum, we proposed a form of civil power consonant with the principles of Christian wisdom, responding to the very nature and to the welfare of people and Princes. Now, after the example of our predecessors, we intend to turn our attention to the Masonic society, to its whole doctrine, to its intentions, acts, and feelings, in order to illustrate more and more this wicked force and stop the spread of this contagious disease.

There are several sects of men which, though different in name, customs, forms, and origin, are identical in aim and sentiment with Masonry. It is the universal center from which they all spring, and to which they all return. Although in our days these seem to no longer care to hide in darkness, but hold their meetings in the full light and under the eyes of their fellow-men and publish their journals openly, yet they deliberate and preserve the habits and customs of secret societies. Nay, there are in them many secrets which are by law carefully concealed not only from the profane, but also from many associated, viz., the last and intimate intentions, the hidden and unknown chiefs, the hidden and secret meetings, the resolutions and methods and means by which they will be carried into execution. Hence the difference of rights and of duties among the members; hence the distinction of orders and grades and the severe discipline by which they are ruled. The initiated must promise, nay, take an oath, that they will never, at any way or at any time, disclose their fellow-members and the emblems by which they are known, or expose their doctrines. So, by false appearance, but with the same kind of simulation, the Masons chiefly strive, as once did the Manichseans, to hide and to admit no witnesses but their own. They seek skillfully hiding places, assuming the appearance of literary men or philosophers, associated for the purpose of erudition; they have always ready on their tongues the speech of cultivated urbanity, and proclaim their charity toward the poor; they look for the improvement of the masses, to extend the benefits of social comfort to as many of mankind as possible. Those purposes, though they may be true, yet are not the only ones. Besides, those who are chosen to join the society must promise and swear to obey the leaders and teachers with great respect and trust; to be ready to do whatever is told them, and accept death and the most horrible punishment if they disobey. In fact, some who have betrayed the secrets or disobeyed an order are punished with death so skillfully and so audaciously that the murder escaped the investigations of the police. Therefore, reason and truth show that the society of which we speak is contrary to honesty and natural justice.

There are other and clear arguments to show this society is not in agreement with honesty. No matter how great the skill with which men conceal, it is impossible that the cause should not appear in its effects. "A good tree cannot yield bad fruits, nor a bad tree good ones." (Matt. vii., 18.) Masonry generates bad fruits mixed with great bitterness. From the evidence above mentioned we find its aim, which is the desire of overthrowing all the religious and social orders introduced by Christianity, and building a new one according to its taste, based on the foundation and laws of naturalism.

What we have said or will say must be understood of Masonry in general and of all like societies, not of the individual members of the same. In their number there may be not a few who, though they are wrong in giving their names to these societies, yet are neither guilty of their crimes nor aware of the final goal which they strive to reach. Among the associations also, perhaps, some do not approve the extreme conclusions which, as emanating from common principles, it would be necessary to embrace if their deformity and vileness would not be too repulsive. Some of them are equally forced by the places and times not to go so far as they would go or others go; and yet they are not to be considered less Masonic for that, because the Masonic alliance has to be considered not only from actions and deeds, but from general principles.

Now, it is the principle of naturalists, as the name itself indicates, that human nature and human reason in everything must be our teacher and guide. Having once settled this, they are careless of duties toward God, or they pervert them with false opinions and errors. They deny that anything has been revealed by God; they do not admit any religious dogma and truth but what human intelligence can comprehend; they do not allow any teacher to be believed on his official authority. Now, it being the special duty of the Catholic Church, and her duty only, to keep the doctrines received from God and the authority of teaching with all the heavenly means necessary to salvation and preserve them integrally incorrupt, hence the attacks and rage of the enemies are turned against her.

Now, if one watches the proceedings of the Masons, in respect of religion especially, where they are more free to do what they like, it will appear that they carry faithfully into execution the tenets of the naturalists. They work, indeed, obstinately to the end that neither the teaching nor the authority of the Church may have any influence; and therefore they preach and maintain the full separation of the Church from the State. So law and government are wrested from the wholesome and divine virtue of the Catholic Church, and they want, therefore, by all means to rule States independent of the institutions and doctrines of the Church.

To drive off the Church as a sure guide is not enough; they add persecutions and insults. Full license is given to attack with impunity, both by words and print and teaching, the very foundations of the Catholic religion; the rights of the Church are violated; her divine privileges are not respected. Her action is restricted as much as possible; and that by virtue of laws apparently not too violent, but substantially made on purpose to check her freedom. Laws odiously partial against the clergy are passed so as to reduce its number and its means. The ecclesiastical revenue is in a thousand ways tied up, and religious associations abolished and dispersed.

But the war wages more ardently against the Apostolic See and the Roman Pontiff. He was, under a false pretext, deprived of the temporal power, the stronghold of his rights and of his freedom; he was next reduced to an iniquitous condition, unbearable for its numberless burdens until it has come to this, that the Sectarians say openly what they had already in secret devised for a long time, viz., that the very spiritual power of the Pope ought to be taken away, and the divine institution of the Roman Pontificate ought to disappear from the world. If other arguments were needed for this, it would be sufficiently demonstrated by the testimony of many who often, in times bygone and even lately, declared it to be the real supreme aim of the Free-Masons to persecute, with untamed hatred, Christianity, and that they will never rest until they see cast to the ground all religious institutions established by the Pope.

If the sect does not openly require its members to throw away of Catholic faith, this tolerance, far from injuring the Masonic schemes, is useful to them. Because this is, first, an easy way to deceive the simple and unwise ones and it is contributing to proselytize. By opening their gates to persons of every creed they promote, in fact, the great modern error of religious indifference and of the parity of all worships, the best way to annihilate every religion, especially the Catholic, which, being the only true one, cannot be joined with others without enormous injustice.

But naturalists go further. Having entered, in things of greatest importance, on a way thoroughly false, through the weakness of human nature or by the judgment of God, who punishes pride, they run to extreme errors. Thus the very truths which are known by the natural light of reason, as the existence of God, the spirituality and immortality of the soul, have no more consistence and certitude for them.

Masonry breaks on the same rocks by no different way. It is true, Free-Masons generally admit the existence of God; but they admit themselves that this persuasion for them is not firm, sure. They do not dissimulate that in the Masonic family the question of God is a principle of great discord; it is even known how they lately had on this point serious disputes. It is a fact that the sect leaves to the member's full liberty of thinking about God whatever they like, affirming or denying His existence. Those who boldly deny His existence are admitted as well as those, like the Pantheists, admit God but ruin the idea of Him, retaining an absurd caricature of the divine nature, destroying its reality. Now, as soon as this supreme foundation is pulled down and upset, many natural truths must need go down, too, as the free creations of this world, the universal government of Providence, immortality of soul, fixture, and eternal life.

Once having dissipated these natural principles, important practically and theoretically, it is easy to see what will become of public and private morality. We will not speak of supernatural virtues, which, without a special favor and gift of God, no one can practice nor obtain, and of which it is impossible to find a vestige in those who proudly ignore the redemption of mankind, heavenly grace, the sacraments, and eternal happiness. We speak of duties which proceed from natural honesty. Because the principles and sources of justice and morality are these, a God, creator and provident ruler of the world, the eternal law which commands respect and forbids the violation of natural order; the supreme end of man settled a great deal above created things outside of this world. These principles once taken away by the Free-Masons as by the naturalists, immediately natural ethics has no more where to build or to rest. The only morality which Free-Masons admit, and by which they would like to bring up youth, is that which they call civil and independent, or the one which ignores every religious idea. But how poor, uncertain, and variable at every breath of passion is this morality, is demonstrated by the sorrowful fruits which partially already appear. Nay, where it has been freely dominating, having banished Christian education, probity and integrity of manners go down, horrible and monstrous opinions raise their head, and crimes grow with fearful audacity. This is deplored by everybody, and by those who are compelled by evidence and yet would not like to speak so.

Besides, as human nature is infected by original sin and more inclined to vice than to virtue, it is not possible to lead an honest life without mortifying the passions and submitting the appetites to reason. In this fight it is often necessary to despise created good, and undergo the greatest pains and sacrifices in order to preserve to conquering reason its own empire. But naturalists and Masons, rejecting divine revelation, deny original sin, and do not acknowledge that our free will is weakened and bent to evil. To the contrary, exaggerating the strength and excellency of nature, and settling in her the principles and unique rule of justice, they cannot even imagine how, in order to counteract its motions and moderate its appetites, continuous efforts are needed and the greatest constancy. This is the reason why we see so many enticements offered to the passions, journals, and reviews without any shame, theatrical plays thoroughly dishonest; the liberal arts cultivated according to the principles of an impudent realism, effeminate and delicate living promoted by the most refined inventions; in a word, all the entice-ments apt to seduce or weaken virtue carefully practiced things highly to blame, yet becoming the theories of those who take away from man heav-enly goods, and put all happiness in transitory things and bind it to earth.

What we have said may be confirmed by things of which it is not easy to think or to speak. As these shrewd and malicious men do not find more servility and docility than in souls already broken and subdued by the tyr-anny of the passions, there have been in the Masonic sect some who openly said and proposed that the multitudes should be urged by all means and artifice into license, so that they should afterward become an easy instru-ment for the most daring enterprise.

For domestic society the doctrine of almost all naturalists is that mar-riage is only a civil contract, and may be lawfully broken by the will of the contracting parties; the State has power over the matrimonial bond. In the education of the children no religion must be applied, and when grown up every one will select that which he likes.

Now Free-Masons accept these principles without restriction; and not only do they accept them, but they endeavor to act so as to bring them into moral and practical life. In many countries which are professedly Catholic, marriages not celebrated in the civil form are considered null; elsewhere laws allow divorce. In other places everything is done in order to have it permitted. So the nature of marriage will be soon changed and reduced to a temporary union, which can be done and undone at pleasure.

The sect of the Masons aims unanimously and steadily also at the pos-session of the education of children. They understand that a tender age is easily bent, and that there is no more useful way of preparing for the State such citizens as they wish. Hence, in the instruction and education of chil-dren, they do not leave to the ministers of the Church any part either in directing or watching them. In many places they have gone so far that children's education is all in the hands of laymen: and from moral teaching every idea is banished of those holy and great duties which bind together man and God.

The principles of social science follow. Here naturalists teach that men have all the same rights, and are perfectly equal in condition; that every man is naturally independent; that no one has a right to command others; that it is tyranny to keep men subject to any other authority than that which emanates from themselves. Hence the people are sovereign; those who rule have no authority but by the commission and concession of the people; so that they can be deposed, willing or unwilling, according to the wishes of the people. The origin of all rights and civil duties is in the people or in the State, which is ruled according to the new principles of liberty. The State must be godless; no reason why one religion ought to be preferred to another; all to be held in the same esteem.

Now it is well known that Free-Masons approve these maxims, and that they wish to see governments shaped on this pattern and model needs no demonstration. It is a long time, indeed, that they have worked with all their strength and power openly for this, making thus an easy way for those, not a few, more audacious and bold in evil, who meditate the communion and equality of all goods after having swept away from the world every distinction of social goods and conditions.

From these few hints it is easy to understand what is the Masonic sect and what it wants. Its tenets contradict so evidently human reason that nothing can be more perverted. The desire of destroying the religion and Church established by God, with the promise of immortal life, to try to revive, after eighteen centuries, the manners and institutions of paganism, is great foolishness and bold impiety. No less horrible or unbearable is it to repudiate the gifts granted through His adversaries. In this foolish and ferocious attempt, one recognizes that untamed hatred and rage of revenge kindled against Jesus Christ in the heart of Satan.

The other attempt in which the Masons work so much, viz., to pull down the foundations of morality, and become co-operators of those who, like brutes, would see that become lawful which they like, is nothing but to urge mankind into the most abject and ignominious degradation.

This evil is aggravated by the dangers which threaten domestic and civil society. As we have at other times explained, there is in marriage, through the unanimous consent of nations and of ages, a sacred and religious character; and by divine law the conjugal union is indissoluble. Now, if this union is dissolved, if divorce is juridically permitted, confusion and discord must inevitably enter the domestic sanctuary, and woman will lose her dignity and the children every security of their own welfare.

That the State ought to profess religious indifference and neglect God in ruling society, as if God did not exist, is a foolishness unknown to the very heathen, who had so deeply rooted in their mind and in their heart, not only the idea of God, but the necessity also of public worship, that they supposed it to be easier to find a city without any foundation than without any God. And really human society, from which nature has made us, was instituted by God, the author of the same nature, and from Him emanates, as from its source and principle, all this everlasting abundance of numberless goods. As, then, the voice of nature tells us to worship God with religious piety, because we have received from Him life and the goods which accompany life, so, for the same reasons, people and States must do the same. Therefore those who want to free society from any religious duty are not only unjust but unwise and absurd.

Once grant that men through God's will are born for civil society, and that sovereign power is so strictly necessary to society that when this fails society necessarily collapses, it follows that the right of command emanates from the same principle from which society itself emanates; hence the reason why the minister of God is invested with such authority. Therefore, so far as it is required from the end and nature of human society, one must obey lawful authority as we would obey the authority of God, supreme ruler of the universe; and it is a capital error to grant to the people full power of shaking off at their own will the yoke of obedience.

Considering their common origin and nature, the supreme end proposed to every one, and the right and duties emanating from it, men no doubt are all equal. But as it is impossible to find in them equal capacity, and as through bodily or intellectual strength one differs from others, and the variety of customs, inclinations, and personal qualities are so great, it is absurd to pretend to mix and unify all this and bring in the order of civil life a rigorous and absolute equality. As the perfect constitution of the human body results from the union and harmony of different parts, which differ in form and uses, but united and each in his own place form an organism beautiful, strong, useful, and necessary to life, so in the State there is an infinite variety of individuals who compose it. If these all equalized were to live each according to his own whim, it would result in a city monstrous and ugly; whereas if distinct in harmony, in degrees of offices, or inclinations, of arts, they co-operate together to the common good, they will offer the image of a city well harmonized and conformed to nature.

The turbulent errors which we have mentioned must inspire governments with fear; in fact, suppose the fear of God in life and respect for divine laws to be despised, the authority of the rulers allowed and authorized would be destroyed, rebellion would be left free to popular passions, and universal revolution and subversion must necessarily come. This subversive revolution is the deliberate aim and open purpose of the numerous communistic and socialistic associations. The Masonic sect has no reason to call itself foreign to their purpose, because Masons promote their designs and have with them common capital principles. If the extreme consequences are not everywhere reached in fact, it is not the merit of the sect nor owing to the will of the members, but of that divine religion which cannot be extinguished, and of the most select part of society, which, refusing to obey secret societies, resists strenuously their immoderate efforts.

May Heaven grant that universally from the fruits we may judge the root, and from impending evil and threatening dangers we may know the bad seed ! We have to fight a shrewd enemy, who, cajoling Peoples and Kings, deceives them all with false promises and fine flattery.

Free-Masons, insinuating themselves under pretence of friendship into the hearts of Princes, aim to have them powerful aids and accomplices to overcome Christianity, and in order to excite them more actively they calumniate the Church as the enemy of royal privileges and power. Having thus become confident and sure, they get great influence in the government of States, resolve yet to shake the foundations of the thrones, and persecute, calumniate, or banish those sovereigns who refuse to rule as they desire.

By these arts flattering the people, they deceive them. Proclaiming all the time public prosperity and liberty; making multitudes believe that the Church is the cause of the iniquitous servitude and misery in which they are suffering, they deceive people and urge on the masses craving for new things against both powers. It is, however, true that the expectation of hoped-for advantages is greater than the reality; and poor people, more and more oppressed, see in their misery those comforts vanish which they might easily and abundantly found in organized Christian society. But the punishment of the proud, who rebel against the order established by the providence of God, is that they find oppression and misery exactly where they expected prosperity according to their desire.

Now, if the Church commands us to obey before all God, the Lord of everything, it would be an injurious calumny to believe her the enemy of the power of Princes and a usurper of their rights. She wishes, on the contrary, that what is due to civil power may be given to it conscientiously. To recognize, as she does, the divine right of command, concedes great dignity to civil power, and contributes to conciliate the respect and love of subjects. A friend of peace and the mother of concord, she embraces all with motherly love, intending only to do good to men, she teaches that justice must be united with clemency, equality with command, law with moderation, and to respect every tight, maintain order and public tranquility, relieve as much as possible public and private miseries. "But," to use the words of St. Augustine, "they believe, or want to make believe, that the doctrine of Gospel is not useful to society, because they wish that the State shall rest not on the solid foundation of virtue, but on impunity of vice."

It would, therefore, be more according to civil wisdom and more necessary to universal welfare that Princes and Peoples, instead of joining the Free-Masons against the Church, should unite with the Church to resist the Free-Masons' attacks.

At all events, in the presence of such a great evil, already too much spread, it is our duty, venerable brethren, to find a remedy. And as we know that in the virtue of divine religion, the more hated by Masons si as it is the more feared, chiefly consists the best and most solid of efficient remedy, we think that against the common enemy one must have recourse to this in wholesome strength. We, by our authority, ratify and confirm all things which the Roman Pontiffs, our predecessors, have ordered to check the purposes and stop the efforts of the Masonic sect, and all these which they establish to keep off or withdraw the faithful from such societies. And here, trusting greatly to the good will of the faithful, we pray and entreat each of them, as they love of their own salvation, to make it a duty of conscience not to depart from what has been on this point prescribed by the Apostolic See.

We entreat and pray you, venerable brethren, who co-operate with us, to root out this poison, which spreads widely among the Nations. It is your duty to defend the glory of God and the salvation of souls. Keeping before your eyes those two ends, you shall lack neither in courage nor in fortitude. To judge which may be the more efficacious means to overcome difficulties and obstacles belongs to your prudence. Yet as we find it agreeable to our ministry to point out some of the most useful means, the first thing to do is to strip from the Masonic sect its mask and show it as it is, teaching orally and by pastoral letters the people about the frauds used by these societies to flatter and entice, the perversity of its doctrines, and the dishonesty of its works. As our predecessors have many times declared, those who love the Catholic faith and their salvation must be sure that they cannot give their names for any reason to the Masonic sect without sin. Let no one believe a simulated honesty. It may seem to some that Masons never impose anything openly contrary to faith or to morals, but as the scope and nature is essentially bad in these sects, it is not allowed to give one's name to them or to help them in any way.

It is also necessary with assiduous sermons and exhortations to arouse in the people love and zeal for religious instruction. We recommend, therefore, that by appropriate declarations, orally and in writing, the fundamental principles of those truths may be explained in which Christian wisdom is entertained. It is only thus that minds can be cured by instruction, and warned against the various forms of error and vice, and the various enticements especially in this great freedom of writing and great desire of learning.

It is a laborious work, indeed, in which you will have associated and companioned your clergy, if properly trained and taught by your zeal. But such a beautiful and important cause requires the co- operating industry of those laymen who unite doctrine and probity with the love of religion and of their country. With the united strength of these two orders endeavor, dear brethren, that men may know and love the Church; because the more their love and knowledge of the Church grows the more they will abhor and fly from secret societies.

Therefore, availing ourselves of this present occasion, we remind you of the necessity of promoting and protecting the Third Order of St. Francis, whose rules, with prudent indulgence, we lately mitigated. According to the spirit of its institution it intends only to draw men to imitate Jesus Christ, to love the Church, and to practice all Christian virtues, and therefore it will prove useful to extinguish the contagion of sects.

May it grow more and more, this holy congregation, from which, among others, can be expected also this precious fruit of bringing minds back to liberty, fraternity, and equality; not those which are the dream of the Masonic sect, but which Jesus Christ brought into this world and Francis revived. The liberty, we say, of the children of God which frees from the servitude of Satan and from the passions, the worst tyrants; the fraternity which emanates from God, the Father and Creator of all; the equality established on justice and charity, which does not destroy among men every difference, but which, from variety of life, offices, and inclinations, makes that accord and harmony which is exacted by nature for the utility and dignity of civil society.

Thirdly, there is an institution wisely created by our forefathers, and by lapse of time abandoned, which in our days can be used as a model and form for something like it. We mean the colleges or corporations of arts and trades associated under the guidance of religion to defend interests and manners, which colleges, in long use and experience, were of great advantage to our fathers, and will be more and more useful to our age, because they are suited to break the power of the sects. Poor workingmen, for besides their condition, deserving charity and relief, they are particularly exposed to the seductions of the fraudulent and deceives. They must, therefore, be helped with the greatest generosity and invited to good societies that they may not be dragged into bad ones. For this reason we would like very much to see everywhere arise, fit for the new times, under the auspices and patronage of the Bishops, these associations, for the benefit of the people. It gives us a great pleasure to see them already established in many places, together with the Catholic patronages; two institutions which aim to help the honest class of workingmen, and to help and protect their families, their children, and keep in them, with the integrity of manners, love of piety and knowledge of religion.

Here we cannot keep silence concerning the society of St. Vincent de Paul, celebrated for the spectacle and example offered and so well deserving of the poor. The works and intentions of that society are well known. It is all for the succor and help of the suffering and poor, encouraging them with wonderful tact and that modesty which the less showy the more is fit for the exercise of Christian charity and the relief of human miseries.

Fourthly, in order more easily to reach the end, we recommend to your faith and watchfulness the youth, the hope of civil society. In the good education of the same place a great part of your care. Never believe you have watched or done enough in keeping youth from those masters from whom the contagious breath of the sect is to be feared. Insist that parents and spiritual directors in teaching the catechism may never cease to admonish appropriately children and pupils of the wicked nature of these sects, that they may also learn in time the various fraudulent arts which their propagators use to entice people. Those who prepare children for first communion will do well if they will persuade them to promise not to give their names to any society without asking their parents' or their pastor's or their confessor's advice.

But we understand how our common labor would not be sufficient to outroot this dangerous seed from the field of the Lord, if the Heavenly Master of the vineyard is not to this effect granting to us His generous help. We must, then, implore His powerful aid with anxious fervor equal to the gravity of the danger and to the greatness of the need. Inebriated by its prosperous success, Masonry is insolent, and seems to have no more limits to its pertinacity. Its sectaries bound by an iniquitous alliance and secret unity of purpose, they go on hand in hand and encourage each other to dare more and more for evil. Such a strong assault requires a strong defence. We mean that all the good must unite in a great society of action and prayers. We ask, therefore, from them two things: On one hand, that, unanimously and in thick ranks, they resist immovably the growing impetus of the sects; on the other, that, raising their hands with many sighs to God, they implore that Christianity may grow vigorous; that the Church may recover her necessary liberty; that wanderers may come again to salvation; that errors give place to truth and vice to virtue.

Let us invoke for this purpose the mediation of Mary, the Virgin Mother of God, that against the impious sects in which one sees clearly revived the contumacious pride, the untamed perfidy, the simulating shrewdness of Satan, she may show her power, she who triumphed over him since the first conception.

Let us pray also St. Michael, the prince of the angelic army, conqueror of the infernal enemy; St. Joseph, spouse of the most Saintly Virgin, heavenly and wholesome patron of the Catholic Church; the great Apostles Peter and Paul, propagators and defenders of the Christian faith. Through their patronage and the perseverance of common prayers let us hope that God will condescend to piously help human society threatened by so many dangers.

As a pledge of heavenly graces and of our benevolence, we impart with great affection to you, venerable brethren, to the clergy and people trusted to your care, the Apostolic benediction.

Given at Rome, near St. Peter, the 20th of April, 1884, the seventh year of our pontificate.

LEO, PP. XIII

ALBERT PIKE'S REPLY TO THE POPE'S LETTER

IF THE Encyclical Letter of Leo XIII, entitled, from its opening words, *Humanum Genus*, had been nothing more than a denunciation of Free-Masonry, I should not have thought it worth replying to. But under the guise of a condemnation of Free-Masonry, and a recital of the enormities and immoralities of the Order, in some respects so absurdly false as to be ludicrous, notwithstanding its malignity, it proved upon perusal to be a declaration of war, and the signal for a crusade, against the rights of men individually and of communities of men as organisms; against the separation of Church and State, and the confinement of the Church within the limits of its legitimate functions; against education free from sectarian religious influences; against the civil policy of non- Catholic countries in regard to marriage and divorce; against the great doctrine upon which, as upon a rock not to be shaken, the foundations of our Republic rest, that "men are superior to institutions, and not institutions to men"; against the right of the people to depose oppressive, cruel and worthless rulers; against the exercise of the rights of free thought and free speech, and against, not only republican, but all constitutional government.

It was the signal for the outbreaking of an already organized conspiracy against the peace of the world, the progress of intellect, the emancipation of humanity, the immunity of human creatures from arrest, imprisonment, torture, and murder by arbitrary power, the right of men to the free pursuit of happiness. It was a declaration of war, arraying all faithful Catholics in the United States, not only against their fellow-citizens, the Brethren of the Order of Free-Masons, but against the principles that are the very life-blood of the government of the people of which they were supposed to be a part, and not the members of Italian Colonies, docile and obedient subjects of a foreign Potentate, and of the Cardinals, European and American, his Princes of the Church.

Therefore, seeing it nowhere replied to in the English language in a manner that seemed to me worthy of Free-Masonry, I undertook to answer it for the Ancient and Accepted Scottish Rite, which has been ever prompt to vindicate itself from aspersion, and carry the war into the quarters of error. I did not propose to stand upon the defensive, protesting against the accusations of the Papal Bull, as unjust to the FreeMasonry of the English-speaking countries of the world, pleading the irresponsibility of British and American Masonry for the acts or opinions of the FreeMasonry of the Continent of Europe: nor was I inclined to apologize for the audacity of Free-Masonry in daring to exist and to be on the side of the great principles of free government.

When the journal in London which speaks for the Free-Masonry of the Grand Lodge of England, deprecatingly protested that the English Masonry was innocent of the charges preferred by the Papal Bull against Free-Masonry as one and indivisible; when it declared that the English Free-Masonry had no opinions political or religious, and that it did not in the least degree sympathize with the loose opinions and extravagant utterances of part of the Continental Free-Masonry, it was very justly and very conclusively checkmated by the Romish organs with the reply: "It is idle for you to protest. You are Free-Masons, and you recognize them as Free- Masons. You give them countenance, encouragement and support, and you are jointly responsible with them and cannot shirk that responsibility."

And here is what is said by the Bishop of Ascalon, Vicar-Apostolic of Bombay, &c., in a pastoral letter promulgating the Bull:

"In the performance of their duty, the Parish Priests and Confessors must not admit as valid or reasonable the common excuse that Free-Masonry in India and England aims at nothing but social amusement, mutual advancement, and charitable benevolence. Such objects require neither a terrible oath of secrecy nor an elaborate system and scale of numerous Degrees, nor a connection with the Masonic Lodges of other countries, about whose anti-Christian, anti-social, and revolutionary character and aim no doubt nor further concealment is possible. The Masonic lodges all over the world are firmly knitted and bound together in solidarity. If all of them share in the pleasure of a triumph achieved by a particular Lodge, or by the Lodges of a particular country, all must likewise submit to the stigma of an anti-Christian, anti-social, and revolutionary sect, as which Free-Masonry is in many countries already openly known, and even unblushingly confessed by its own adepts."

I was not willing that the Ancient and Accepted Scottish Rite in the Southern Jurisdiction of the United States should humiliate itself to as little purpose: nor was there any danger that it would do so.

The organs of our American Masonry were inclined to treat the Encyclical Letter as needing no reply, and to regard it with contemptuous indifference. In their opinion, it seemed, the lightnings of the Vatican were harmless, and the American Masonry would do a foolish thing to pay any attention to the Bull. It may be so; and I receive with due humility the admonition that to reply to it was to make much ado about nothing.

But the Free-Masonry of the United States is not what it was in the days of the Fathers. While it has succeeded, obedient to the impulsion of Bro.'. Richard Vaux, of Pennsylvania, and others, in pretty effectually isolating itself from the Masonry of the rest of the world, other Orders at home unceremoniously jostle it in the struggle for precedence, and it in vain appeals to its antiquity and former prestige to protect it against irreverence. Incalculable harm is being done by Bodies of base origin, whose agents traverse the country soliciting men to receive the counterfeit Degrees which they peddle, selling them by the score for ten or fifteen dollars to any one who will buy, and conferring all in an hour or so, or by administering a single obligation. Rites without claim to be Masonic, teaching nothing, worth nothing, flauntingly advertise their multitudes of Degrees that are nothing but numbers and names; new Orders called Masonic spring up like mushrooms; and even the legitimate Masonry, held responsible for all these nuisances and vagaries, parades its uniforms and gewgaws, collars and jewels, too much in the public view, and has so gained popularity while losing its right to reverence.

Its complacent sense of security may be rudely disturbed by and by. It seems to me that an organized crusade against it by all the Roman Catholics in the United States, an anti-Masonic movement organized and directed by the Papacy, and engineered by Priests, Bishops and Cardinals, is not a thing to be made light of by the American Masonry, treated with indifference and regarded with a lordly and sublime contempt. And it is very certain that its protestations that it has no political or religious opinions, and no sympathies with the revolutionary tendencies of the Masonry of the Continent, will neither placate the Papacy nor win for it respect anywhere.

If, in other countries, Free-Masonry has lost sight of the Ancient Landmarks, even tolerating communism and atheism, it is better to endure ten years of these evils than it would be to live a week under the devilish tyranny of the Inquisition and of the black soldiery of Loyola. Atheism is a dreary unbelief, but it at least does not persecute, torture, or roast men who believes that there is a God. Free-Masonry will not long indulge in extravagances of opinion or action anywhere It has within itself the energy and capacity to free itself in time of all errors: and he greatly belittle Humanity who proclaims it to be unsafe to let Error say what it will, if Truth is free to combat and confute it. But Free- Masonry will effect its reforms in its own proper way; and would not resort, if it could, not even to save itself from dissolution, to means like those which the Papacy has heretofore employed, and would gladly employ again, to extirpate Judaism, Heresy and Free- Masonry.

Nowhere in the world has Free-Masonry ever conspired against any Government entitled to its obedient or to men's respect. Wherever now there is a Constitutional Government which respects the rights of me and of the people and the public opinion of the worlds it is the loyal supporter of that Government. It has never taken pay from armed Despotism, or abetts persecution. It has fostered no Borgias; no stranglers or starvers to death of other Popes, like Boniface VII no poisoners, like Alexander VI and Paul III. It has no roll of beatified Inquisitors or other murderers; as it has never, in any country, been the enemy of the people, the suppresser of scientific truth, the stifler of the God-given right of free inquiry as to the great problems, intellectual and spiritual, presented by the Universe, the extorter of confession by the rack, the burner of women and of the exhumed bodies of the dead. It has never been the enemy of the human race, and the curse and dread of Christendom. Its patron Saints have always been St. John the Baptist and St. John the Evangelist, and not Pedro Arbues d'Epila, Principal Inquisitor of Zaragoza, who, slain in 1485, was beatified by Alexander VII in 1664.

It is not when the powers of the Papacy are concentrated to crush the Free-Masonry of the Latin Kingdoms and Republics of the world, that the Masons of the Ancient and Accepted Scottish Rite in the United States will, from any motive whatever, proclaim that they have no sympathy with the Masons of the Continent of Europe, or with those of Mexico or of the South American Republics. If these fall into errors of practice or indulge in extravagances of dogma, we will dissent and remonstrate; but we will not forget that the Free-Masonry of our Rite and of the French Rite has always been the Apostle of Civil and Religious Liberty, and that the blood of Spanish and other Latin FreeMasons has again and again glorified and sanctified the implements of torture, the scaffold and the stake, of the Papacy and the Inquisition.

Neither does Free-Masonry any more execrate the atrocities of the Papacy than it does those of Henry VIII of England and his daughter Elizabeth, the murder of Sir Thomas More and that of Servetus, and those of the Quakers put to death by bigotry in New England; than the cruel torturing and slaying of Covenanters and Non-Conformists, the ferocities of Claverhouse and Kirk, and the pitiless slaughtering of Catholic Priests by the revolutionary fury of France.

It well knows and cheerfully acknowledges the services which some of the Roman Pontiffs and a multitude of its clergy have in the past centuries rendered to Humanity. It has always done ample justice to their pure lives, their good deeds, their self-denial, their devotedness, their unostentatious heroism, as these have been eloquently and beautifully portrayed by Kenelm Henry Digby. It has always done full justice to the memories of the faithful and devoted Missionaries of the Order of Jesus and others, who bore the Cross into every barbarous land under the sun, to make known to savages the truths and errors taught by the Roman Church, and the simpler arts of civilization. It was never the unreasoning and insensate reviler of that church, railing against it without measure or regard to justice and truth; nor could it be, remembering that lot only Bayard and Du Guesclin, but Sir Henry More, Las Casas and Fenelon were loyal servants of it.

But also it has known to its cost that none of the stages of the History of the World are more full of rightful crimes and monstrous acts of cruel outrage than those of the Papacy of Rome; and it now knows, by the revival of the Bulls of Benedict and Clement, that the seeming moderation, mildness and liberality of opinion of that Church have been but a mask, which, being torn from its face, its intolerant, persecuting, cruel, inhuman spirit flames out as ferociously as ever from its bloody eyes.

It seems to have learned nothing, and to be incapable of learning anything, although a higher will and a sterner law than its own have made it powerless to burn heretics, whether men or women, free-thinkers and Free-Masons, at the stake, or to extort confessions of guilt by torture; and permit it no longer to persecute science as heresy and blasphemy.

For surely if the age of the Papacy had brought with it a larger measure of wisdom, as men were fondly hoping, the present Pope would not, at this age of the world, have ordered every Catholic in every Republic in the world to become not only disloyal to but the irreconcilable enemy of the Government under which he lives.

Nor would the present Pope have re-enacted and made his own the Bulls of Benedict and Clement, or have pronounced against Catholics who persist in continuing to be Free-Masons, all the lesser and greater penalties ever prescribed by any of his predecessors. For (not to multiply appalling instances) he cannot be ignorant that, at the first *auto da fe*, ("Act of the Faith,") celebrated at Valladolid in Spain, on the 21st of May, 1559, and at the second even more solemn one, held in the same city in the presence of Philip II himself, his son and sister, the Prince of Parma, and many Grandees and Nobles of Spain and high ladies of the Court and country, there were strangled and then burned, for the unpardonable sin of having become convinced of the truth of, and therefore having embraced, some of the opinions of Martin Luther, Dona Beatrix de Vibero Cazalla and nine other women, in presence of the audience; and at the first, the body of Dona Eleonora de Vibero, (who had been interred as a Catholic, without suspicion ever having been raised as to her orthodoxy, and when she had, in her last sickness, taken all the sacraments,) having been exhumed, was borne to the pyre on a bier, adorned with a San Benito of flames, the pasteboard mitre on its head, and so burned. Upon the confession extracted from some prisoners under the tortures, or by threats of torture, the Fiscal of the Inquisition had accused her, after her burial, of Lutheranism, for permitting her house to be used for Lutheran assemblings; whereupon she was adjudged by the beloved Tribunal of the Papacy to have died in heresy, her memory was condemned to infamy entailed on her posterity, and her property confiscated, her body ordered to be exhumed and burned, her house razed to the ground, and forbidden to be rebuilded, and a monument was ordered to be set up on the site with an inscription relating to this event.

Even the impudence of a Roman Catholic journalist will hardly venture to stigmatize this as false. It is related by Juan Antonio Llorente, in his *Critical History of the Inquisition in Spain*, derived from original documents in the archives of the Supreme Tribunal and those of the Subterranean Tribunals of the Holy Office: from which came the statements contained in our "Reply" of the number of victims butchered by Torquemada and his successors. Llorente was ex-Secretary of the Inquisition of the Court, Canon of the

Primatical Church of Toledo, Chancellor of the University of that city, Knight of the Order of Charles III, and member of the Royal Academies of History and of the Spanish Language at Madrid.

"All these dispositions" (of the judgment against the dead woman Eleonora) "were executed," Llorente says: "I have seen the place, the column and the inscriptions. It is stated that this monument of human ferocity against the dead was demolished in 1809."

But at these autos da fe the Archbishops and Bishops, clergy, nobles, and ladies present were not entirely deprived of the expected luxury and pleasure of seeing human creatures burned alive. At the first, Francisco de Vibero Cazalla and the Licentiate Antonio Herrezuelo, and at the second, Don Carlos de Seso and Juan Sanchez, were roasted alive for the mortal sin of Lutheranism. Of a score or two of suspected Lutherans and others, not burned alive, or strangled and then burned, all the property they possessed was confiscated to the uses of the Holy Office, a method of enriching itself which it had then pursued with great diligence, by continual confiscations, for eighty years, and yet was not weary.

At the second, Dona Marina de Guevara, a Nun, accused of Lutheranism, suffered. The Supreme Tribunal decreed that she was guilty, and had incurred the penalty of the greater excommunication, and "remitted" her "to the judicial power and to the secular arm" of the Corregidor and his Lieutenant, "to whom," the judgment said, "we recommend to treat her with kindness and pity," that Tribunal knowing that sentence of death must inevitably and necessarily follow, and that its own judgment was really the death-sentence. If the Corregidor had dared to mitigate the penalty, he would himself have felt fastened into his flesh the sharp and venomous fangs of the Inquisition, for he would have proven himself a favorer of heretics. What a hideous formula was that recommendation to kindness and pity! "It is impossible," Llorente says, "to impose on God by formulas contrary to the secret dispositions of the heart."

"Since the Inquisition was established," Llorente wrote in 1817, "there has hardly been a man celebrated for his knowledge who has not been persecuted as a heretic"; and he gives a formidable list of those who suffered in their liberty, honor and fortune "because they would not shamefully adopt scholastic opinions or erroneous systems born in the ages of ignorance and of barbarism."

Certainly the restoration of this convenient instrument of the Apostolic See, which acts on anonymous denunciations, takes testimony ex parte upon such denunciations, and convicts on suspicions, and confessions extorted by an admirable variety of tortures, and even upon persistent refusals to confess, is not impossible; because, on the 21st of July, 1814, Ferdinand VII reestablished it in Spain, after Bonaparte had suppressed it in 1808, and the Cortes-General Extraordinary of Spain had done the same on the 12th of

February, 1813.

The time may even come again, if Constitutional Government can be destroyed by the Papacy in Spain, Portugal or Italy, when that may happen to a FreeMason, which happened to Gaspardo de Santa Cruz and his son under Ferdinand and Isabella, about the year 1487. The father had taken refuge at Toulouse, in France, where he died, after he had been burned in effigy at Zaragoza. One of his sons was arrested by order of the Inquisitors for having aided the escape of his father. He underwent the punishment of the public auto da fe, and was condemned to take a copy of the judgment rendered against his father, to go to Toulouse and present this copy to the Dominicans, demanding that his father's body should be exhumed and burned; and, finally, to return to Zaragoza and make report to the Inquisitors of the execution of the sentence. And to this shameful, revolting, and monstrous judgment he submitted without murmuring, and executed it.

In 1524 (Charles V being then Emperor of the Romans) there was put up, in the Inquisition at Sevilla, by the Licentiate de la Cueva, by the order and at the cost of the Emperor, an inscription in Latin, composed by Diego de Cortegana, by which it was stated that, from the time of the establishment of the Inquisition there, in 1485, under the Pontificate of Sextus IV and during the reign of Ferdinand V and Isabella, until 1524, "more than two thousand persons obstinate in heresy had been delivered to the flames, after having been judged conformably to law, with the approbation and favor of Innocent VIII, Alexander VI, Pius III, Julius II, Leo X, Adrian VI, and Clement VII."

The Church of Rome had prepared and matured all its plans of campaign against liberal institutions and Constitutional Government, carefully, thoroughly, and comprehensively, before the Encyclical Letter *Humanum Genus* gave the signal for opening the campaign and commencing the new crusade, to endanger the peace of the world, foment anarchy, and initiate a new era of violence and murder. A clerical victory at the elections in Belgium has been followed by the enactment of a law destructive of the common school system, and placing education under the control of the Priests and Jesuits. It will not disturb the Pope or his Cardinal-Princes if civil war results, as now seems probable, if thousands of lives are sacrificed, if the King loses his throne, and the Kingdom of Belgium is obliterated. In Spain the Romish clergy have set on foot a demonstration in every Church throughout the realm in favor of the temporal power of the Pope; and if Alfonso does not place himself unreservedly in the hands and at the bidding of the Church, revolutionary movements against his throne, already beginning to appear in the north of Spain, will be fomented. The Pope promulgates an Encyclical Letter against the adoption of a new law of divorce by the legislative power of France, and instructs the Bishops to annul it so far as they may find it possible. And we may look for disturbances in Mexico and the South

American States, fomented by the Priesthood in obedience to the orders issued from the Vatican against Free-Masons and Constitutional Government.

By Papal Brief of January 17, 1750, the Father Joseph Torrubia, Pro-Censor and Reviser of the Inquisition, was authorized to procure initiation into Masonry, to take all the oaths that might be required of him, and to use every means possible to acquire the most complete knowledge of the membership of the Free-Masonry of Spain: and in March, 1751, the Father Torrubia, having taken without sinfulness the oaths required, and been initiated, put into the hands of the Grand Inquisitor the ninety-seven lists of membership of the ninety-seven Lodges at that time in activity in Spain: upon which, on the 2d of July, 1751, the King, Ferdinand VI, decreed the complete suppression of the Masonic Order, and prescribed the punishment of death, without any form of preliminary procedure, against all who should be convicted of belonging to it.

Undoubtedly Pope Leo XIII would consider it laudable for any good Catholic now, if need were, to imitate the example of the Father Joseph Torrubia; and entirely proper for himself to grant such a brief as was granted to that worthy Father; although all honest men ought to regard such a service as base and infamous, and consider perjury and betrayal of confidence to be virtues only in the eyes of the Church and not in those of God.

But his Apostolic Holiness has graciously permitted that during one year, those who in obedience to his orders renounce Masonry, shall not be required to divulge the names of their superiors in the Order; not because to do so would be unutterable baseness, but because it is politic, as likely to induce many to renounce the Order, who would not be willing to do that and at the same time become faithless and perjured scoundrels.

While inciting the fanatical and venal instruments of his Priesthood against Free-Masonry and Constitutional Government, the Pope omits nothing to make more effectual his edict of Excommunication. It is necessary to give assurance to those who may help in the good work of exterminating Free-Masonry, overturning Constitutional Government, and re-enslaving intellects, souls and science, of immunity, if not in this world, then certainly in the next, for all the outrages, villainies and crimes that they may commit.

Accordingly the Pope embraces the present occasion, while he is causing disturbances in Belgium, Spain, Mexico and Italy, to issue his proclamation, as Spiritual Autocrat of the whole world, panoplied with all the powers of the Almighty God, by which he plenarily pardons all the sins of a great number of the faithful, neither knowing nor caring what the enormity of those sins may be.

The paragraphs which follow, taken from a translation in the Catholic Examiner of Brooklyn, of the Encyclical Letter of Leo XIII, of August 30, 1884, "setting apart October as a month of prayer to the Mother of God," will show that we do not misunderstand the use to which the Pope puts his plenary indulgences:

"For it is, indeed, an arduous and exceedingly weighty matter that is now in hand; it is to humiliate an old and most subtle enemy in the spread-out array of his power; to win back the freedom of the Church and of her Head; to preserve and secure the fortifications within which should rest in peace the safety and weal of human society.

The letter then proceeds to state the materialistic "principles of statesmanship." It says: "They maintain that all things are vested in a free people; that power is held by the order or permission of that people, so that, if the popular pleasure change, Princes may be degraded from their rank even against their will. They assert that the source of all laws and civil duties is either in the multitude, or in the power that rules the State, and this when formed by the newest teaching." And the Letter avers, "that these very sentiments are equally pleasing to the FreeMasons; and that they wish to arrange States after this likeness and pattern, is too well known to need demonstration. For long indeed they have been openly working for this object with all their strength and resources."

These are the political principles of all English-speaking Masons; not because they are Free-Masons, not because these principles are taught in their lodges for they teach nothing there in regard to politics or systems of government; but because they are Englishmen, Scotsmen, Irishmen, or citizens of the United States; and their Civil Governments are founded upon these principles. In other countries these are the principles which have always inspired the Ancient and Accepted Scottish Rite, and the French or Modern Rite; and these Rites have therefore always been the advocates and champions, especially in the Latin countries of Europe, of freedom and constitutional government; and in this chiefly consist their glory and their honor. The Roman Catholic Church has been always and everywhere on the side of the arbitrary power Princes and Potentates: Masonry on the side of the people. Thou hast said truly, O Pope!

Then the Successor of Saint Peter thus announces to the Faithful the law by which they are to be absolutely governed, - the law of the Divine right of anointed Princes:

"As men are born by the will of God for civil union and association, and as the power of ruling is so necessary a bond of civil society, that on its removal that society must suddenly be severed, it follows that He who gave birth to society gives birth also to the rule of authority. Whence it is understood that he in whom power is, WHOEVER HE IS, is God's Minister. Wherefore, so far as the end and nature of human society require, it is as right to obey lawful authority, when it issues just orders as it is to obey the power of God who rules all things: and this is pre-eminently inconsistent with truth, that it should depend upon the will of the people to cast off obedience at its pleasure."

Is every one, then, who finds himself actually possessing power, thereby God's Minister? Was Cromwell God's Minister? Was William of Orange God's Minister? Was Napoleon the Great? Were William and Mary God's Ministers? Are the King and Parliament of Italy God's Ministers? Are the Emperors of Germany and Brazil God's Ministers? Oh no! The Pope means those in whom power is, they having lawful authority, i. e., those whose rule and power are sanctioned by the Church. How, according to his doctrine, if it be "pre-eminently inconsistent with truth" that the people may rid a country of a ferocious and brutal tyrant, by compelling his abdication - of a Ferdinand VII, or Philip II, (whose will and that of the Church of Rome Alva executed in the Netherlands, leaving written there all over the land the never-to-be-effaced records of the blood-guiltiness of the Church and King), - of a Bomba, of a Nero, of a Caligula, of a Borgia, - how is any bloody and brutal miscreant, wearing the purple, to be dethroned? Must the people endure until God shall remove the butchering malefactor by death, that perhaps Commodus may succeed Tiberius, or a worse and meaner tyrant follow Bomba?

There must be some power on earth to set free a suffering people. It must not "depend upon the will of the people to cast off obedience at its pleasure, - all Catholics are ordered to believe." When, then? When the Church may authorize it; when the Pope may declare the Throne forfeited for crime, and excommunicate the Ruler, as Heretic or Free-Mason? Is it not this that is meant?

Thus the Pope pronounces by his prerogative of infallibility, and as Vicegerent of God, whom it is as unlawful to refuse to obey as it is to refuse "to obey the power of God who rules all things," that the dethronement of James II, Catholic King of England, was an act of disobedience of the power of God.

"On the contempt for the authority of Princes, on the allowing and approving of lust for sedition, on the granting of full license to the passions of the people, bridled only by the fear of punishment, there must of necessity arise a change and overthrow of all things."

The Free-Masons, he passionately cries, "have begun to have great weight in ruling States, but they are ready to shake the foundations of Empires, and to censure, accuse and drive out the chief men of a State, whenever its administration seems different from their wishes. Just so have they deluded the people by their flattery. By calling in sounding terms for liberty and public prosperity, and saying that it is owing to the Church and Princes that the people are not delivered from unjust slavery and want, they have imposed upon the populace, and have instigated it by a thirst for revolution to attack the power of both."

Where? Garibaldi, in Italy, was a Free-Mason, and there are perhaps a hundred and fifty Masonic lodges in Italy; and yet a King rules peacefully there, upheld by the Free-Masons, his Minister, Depretis, being a Mason. In

Brazil the Emperor is a Free-Mason of the 33d Degree, and there have been no insurrections or disturbances of the public peace there, though the Free-Masons assemble in some two hundred Lodges and higher Bodies. In Portugal there are a Grand Orient and Supreme Council and sixty or seventy Lodges, and the Marshal Duke Saldanha, why by peaceful revolution gave that Kingdom a constitutional government, was Ex-Grand Master of Masons; and yet a King reigns peacefully in Portugal. In Spain there are two hundred Lodges, and Sagasta is a Free-Mason, and Alfonso reigns secure, his throne upheld by FreeMasonry.

Attacks upon the Church and Princes, the Pope exclaims, instigated by Free-Masons, have given the people greater expectation than reality of advantage. "Nay, rather, the common people, suffering worse oppression, are for the most part forced to be without those very alleviations of their miseries, which they would find with ease and abundance, if matters were arranged according to Christian ordinances. But as many as strive against the order arranged by divine Providence, usually pay this penalty for their pride, that they meet with a wretched and miserable fortune in the quarter whence they rashly expected prosperity and success."

The Spanish Colonies in the New World threw off by revolt the intolerable yoke of oppression of the Spanish Crown, and made themselves free Republics. They were not content with "matters arranged according to Christian Ordinances" by the Catholic Church, for the benefit of a rapacious and cruel government, with those "Ordinances" administered by Inquisitors. Are the people of Mexico loosers thereby? Are those of Chile, or Venezuela? The Netherlands, bled nearly unto death, at last, by heroic endurance and matchless courage, rescued their country from the Satanic rule of Alva. France put an end to such Saturnalia of Hell there as that of the Eve of St. Bartholomew, and in carrying away the Pope to Avignon paid Rome in full for the blood with which the grey hairs of old Coligni dabbled the stones of Paris. God, by the instrumentality of Luther, avenged the murdered Albigenses and Lollards, Huss and Wiclif, Jerome of Prague and Savonarola; seriously disarranging "matters arranged according to Christian Ordinances." Has all this been to the manifest disadvantage of the people of the liberated countries of the world ? Have the Netherlands, Belgium, Portugal, Italy, lost by it? Is France miserable and suffering? Is Germany wretched? Does Great Britain languish for want of the tender mercies of the Papacy?

That great Statesman, Edmund Burke, said that he did not know how to draw an indictment against a whole people; but we have thus shown, by the very words, faithfully translated, of the Roman Pontiff himself, that this Encyclical Letter, which purports to be only an arraignment and condemnation of Free-Masonry, is in its principal intent and deepest significance an indictment, not only of the people of every Republic and Constitutional Monarchy in the world; but of every Protestant country in the world; and not only of the people of every Protestant country in the world, but of all that portion of the people of every Catholic country who have in these later centuries asserted the right of the people to have a voice in the affairs of government, and to be secure in their persons and lives against the infernal methods of procedure, the creation of imaginary crimes, and the cruel torturings upon mere suspicion, of such tribunals as the Inquisition. It is a sentence purporting to be uttered by the voice of God, outlawing and excluding from Heaven all the patriots and lovers of liberty and liberators of the people, all the array of martyrs who have died in endeavoring to vindicate the right of Humanity to freedom of thought and conscience.

It denounces as wicked and criminal, and contrary to the ordinances of the Christian religion, not only the laws which permit the solemnization of marriage by the civil magistrate, and those which exclude sectarian religious teaching from schools and seminaries maintained by public taxation; not only the constitutional provisions which in all the States of these United States decree the separation of Church and State, and refuse to the Church any part in the civil government of the country; not only those by which the pretensions of the Churches and their right to dictate opinions may be freely discussed by the public press; but also the great principle on which the governments of all Republics are founded, of the sovereignty of the people, the only legitimate source and author of civil power and government. It asserts the divine right of Princes, if held by the Church of Rome to have lawful authority, to govern men against their will; that they are the Ministers of God; and that the people have no power to free themselves from the tyranny and oppression of these divinely commissioned scourges and Assassins of Humanity.

It is an indictment of Humanity itself, for its instinctive struggles to lift itself above the miseries and indignities of bodily and intellectual bondage to Priest and Potentate; for the involuntary and irrepressible aspirations of its Soul towards light and knowledge and the free atmosphere of intellectual expansion; and for the not more involuntary quiverings of its tortured, racked, wrenched and mutilated muscles and nerves. It is an indictment of Civilization, of Progress, of the Spirit of Manhood, of the self-respect of the Peoples, of the Progress onward and upward of Humanity, of the Spirit of the Age, which is the very Inspiration of God; and of God Himself and the beneficent Providence of God, Who loves the people in rags, hungry and hopeless, better than He loves the Priests in scarlet and the Tyrants in purple.

In renewing and by his Apostolic authority confirming everything decreed by former Popes against Free-Masonry, ratifying their Bulls as well in general as in particular, Leo XIII leaves to his faithful subjects no discretionary power to regard any portions of those anathemas as obsolete, or to pay respect and obedience to those laws, Bills of Right, or Constitutions, of the countries in which they live, which may forbid the enforcement of the com-

114

mands of the Church containing these Bulls.

For he immediately adds: "Having entire confidence in this respect, in the good will of those who are Christians, we beseech them, in the name of their eternal salvation, and we demand of them to make it for themselves a sacred obligation of conscience, never to depart, even by one single line, from the mandates promulgated on this subject by the Apostolic See."

He then proceeds to direct by what measures and devices the Clergy "are "to cause to disappear the impure contagion of the poison which circulates in the veins of society, and infects it throughout."

First: by tearing off the mask of Free-Masonry and showing it as it is.

Second: by special discourses and pastoral letters to instruct the people. "Remind the people," he says, "that by virtue of the decrees often issued by our predecessors, no Catholic, if he desires to continue worthy of the name, and to have for his salvation the concern which it deserves, can, under any pretext, affiliate with the Sect of Free-Masons."

Then, by frequent instruction and exhortation to help the masses to acquire a knowledge of religion, expounding, in writing and orally, the elements of the sacred principles which constitute the Christian philosophy; and so to increase the devotion of Clergy and Laity to the Catholic Church, the result whereof will be increased disgust for secret societies, and greater care to avoid them. To which method of inculcating what is believed by the Church to be truth, and opposing the progress of what it believes to be error, a Free-Mason will be the last man in the world to object, if it is not to be supplemented by other too well known methods.

And, to engage with great zeal in increasing and strengthening the Third Order of Saint Francis, in the discipline whereof the Pope claims to have made wise modifications; so that "it may be able to render greater service in helping to overcome the contagion of these detestable Sects."

Third: to re-engage in establishing corporation of workingmen, to protect, under the tutorship of religion, the interests of labor and the morals of workers; with societies of patrons, to assist and instruct the proletaires, such as is the Society of Saint Vincent de Paul.

Fourth: vigilantly to watch with pastoral solicitude over the young, drawing them away, by renewed efforts, from the schools and teachers where they would be exposed to breathe the poisoned breath of the Sects: parents, teachers and curates, urged by the Bishops, guarding their children and pupils against "these criminal societies," which are ever endeavoring to ensnare them; those who have it in charge to prepare young persons to receive the sacraments, inducing every one of them to take a firm resolution not to join any society without the knowledge of their parents, or without having consulted their curate or confessor.

For the rest, to implore the aid of the Lord, with great ardor and reiterated solicitations, proportioned to the necessity of the circumstances, and the intensity of the peril.

"Haughty on account of its former success, the Sect of Free-Masons insolently erects its head, and its audacity no longer seems to know any bounds. United to one another by the bond of a criminal federation, and by their secret plans, its adepts lend to each other mutual support, and incite each other to dare and to do evil."

"To which violent attack an energetic defence must respond. Good men must unite, and form an immense coalition of prayers and efforts. Especially the Virgin Mary, Mother of God, must be besought to become the auxiliary and interpreter of the Church, displaying her power against the Sects which are reviving the rebellious spirit, the incorrigible perfidy, and the cunning, of the Devil. Saint Michael who precipitated the revolted Angels into hell, Saint Joseph, husband of the Virgin, and the great Apostles Saint Peter and Saint Paul, must also be enlisted: and thus the imminent danger to the human race may be averted."

Instructions of the people in religious doctrine; enlargement of the Third Order of Franciscans; organization of associations of working men; gaining control of the education of the young; and incessant prayer, - these are to be the ostensible means of offense and defence. *A la bonne heure!* If no more were meant. But the Church of Rome has never been in the habit of making known the real means or instruments which it has determined to use for the suppression of heresy or to repress the struggles of Humanity to escape from the intolerable burdens of oppression; and it is not likely to do it now. The ostentatious recital of these peaceful means of antagonism does not agree with the explicit re-enactments of the Bulls of Clement and Benedict. The Church has other measures in view than teaching and prayer; and it is already using them in Belgium and Brazil. It has mysteries the divulgation of which is interdicted; Conclaves and Consistories, Generals of the Order, Assemblies that are secret, as their decisions and the means and agents of execution are. The adepts blindly and without discussion obey the injunctions of their Chiefs, holding themselves always ready, upon the slightest notification or hardly perceptible sign, to execute the orders given them, devoting themselves in advance, in case of disobedience, to the most terrible penalties, and even to death; were the order even to bring about the murder of another William the Silent, or of the Chiefs of a Republic.

With such a Past as that of the Church of Rome is, it would have been wise not to provoke comment upon its real crimes by accusing others of having committed imaginary ones; or exposure of the doctrines of the Jesuits, by libelling those of Free-Masonry.

It is not only just and fair and reasonable, but of absolute necessity, to conclude that any one who speaks to men by authority intends the consequences that may naturally, anywhere, be the effects of his words. It is even of absolute necessity, sometimes, to conclude that ambiguous phrases and significant suggestions and veiled meanings, when used as they are here, are employed to induce the commission of infamies, the explicit incitation whereunto might startle the conscience of Humanity. And this is especially of unavoidable necessity, in the interpretation of the mandates of the Church of Rome against those whom it considers its enemies. For it has never yet repudiated and condemned the maxims of the Spanish Jesuits, or declared the suppression of the Truth or the suggestion of Falsehood, for the benefit of the Church, to be contrary to the spirit of the Gospel, or confessed itself ashamed for having so long employed the infernal enginery of the Inquisition. It is infallible, can never have erred, can never change. It long ago lost all right to expect the world to give it credit for honesty of intention or frankness of expression.

This new Proclamation of Interdict and Excommunication is, it is probable, more especially intended as a political manifesto to the Clergy and Catholics of Italy, Spain, Portugal, Belgium and Brazil, inciting them to treasonable plottings and combinations against the Constitutional Governments of those countries. It preaches to them a new Crusade, the purpose whereof is to destroy those governments, to depose the Monarchs who permit the existence of Free-Masonry in their dominions and the expression of the voice of the people in public affairs; and to place in those Kingdoms the education of the young in the hands of the soldiery of Loyola, and the power of persecuting Free-Masonry and Heresy and the favoring of liberal government in the Holy Office or Inquisition, armed with all its old inhuman and unchristian powers, against which the sense of justice of the whole world long ago revolted. In Brazil it incites the Arch-Bishop of Rio de Janeiro and the Bishop of Para, and all the Jesuits and Ultramontane Clergy, to renew the war a few years ago waged by them against Free-Masonry, against the Emperor and Parliament, and the Laws of the Empire, acting towards the Emperor as towards one excommunicated, reprobated and accursed.

Thus it menaces the public peace in those countries, inciting revolt and insurrection and assassination, and makes the Lord's Prayer the patent of an Inquisitor, and the Sermon on the Mount a warrant for murder.

Already the General of the Jesuits and the Chief Inquisitor of the Holy Office have promulgated their orders to their troops and officials, commanding them to use their utmost exertions to carry into effect the mandates of the Encyclical Letter. In Spain and Portugal secret Anti-Masonic Associations are already being organized under these orders, and like organizations may be looked for in the United States, with resort to every other means of warfare against the great principles which Free-Masonry represents, that can be prudently and safely employed.

It is also a political manifesto, and more, for our neighboring Republic of Mexico, and those of Central and South America. There are Grand Lodges and Supreme Councils of Masons in most of them; and in all, Masonry is free to exist and work undisturbed, and is powerful and influential. In Mexico, the Ex-President, now President Elect of the Republic, and the Actual President, are 33ds, members of the Supreme Council of Mexico created by us, as the President Comonfort was a 33d, Grand Commander of that Supreme Council, and as the President Juarez was a Mason. It is well known that the population at large of the Republic is uneducated and grossly ignorant, and slavishly subservient to the Priesthood; and that it detests and hates Protestants as heretics, damned by the anathemas of the Church, and unfit to live. The Priesthood in Mexico has always been the uncompromising and wily enemy of every patriotic President, of Republican Government, of Free-Masonry, of the principles on which Constitutional Governments are founded, and of all the men by whose sublime efforts and sacrifices Mexico was made and has been maintained a Republic.

It is also well known that, in consequence of the friendly relations between our two Republics, and the extension of railroads in Mexico, built by the capital of our citizens, there now are in that country a great number of citizens of the United States, many of whom have purchased mines and lands, and are working and cultivating them. The Letter *Humanum Genus* is so framed and worded as to be calculated, and must therefore be taken to be artfully and deliberately intended, to incite the Priesthood in Mexico to renewed zeal against heresy and heretics, and more persistent and continuous and better organized and more audacious efforts to destroy Free-Masonry there, and overturn Republicanism. If citizens of the United States peaceably engaged there in useful avocations, should be assassinated by mobs, instigated, if not openly led, by the Priests; if Diaz and Gonzales and other Free-Masons should be murdered, and the Church should inaugurate a bloody civil war, Pope Leo XIII will not be able, by any special pleading, to avoid the responsibility for all the fatal consequences that may ensue.

For men have not forgotten that Ignatious Loyola, founder of the Order of Jesus, promulgated this law.

"Visum est nobis in Domino nullas Constitutiones posse obligationem ad peccatum mortale vel veniale inducere, nisi Superior, (in nomine J.-C. vel in virtute obedientiae,) juberet."

"It has seemed to us in the Lord that on Constitutions can make it obligatory to commit a mortal or a pardonable sin unless the Superior (in the name of Jesus Christ, or in virtue of obedience,) may so order."

No doubt the General of the Jesuits holds the same doctrine today, and is ready to apply it, if occasion should demand, - that the Superior in the Order has the power to command an inferior to commit a mortal sin. It is a fruitful and convenient doctrine, when the matter in hand is to destroy Constitutional Governments in Catholic countries.

There is still more to be considered by the people of the United States; which, when they come fully to comprehend the puport of this manifesto from the Vatican, they will consider. The Catholics, whom it proposes to organize into Italian Colonies or Camps here, obeying the laws enacted at Rome, regulating their political action by principles hostile to those on which Republican Government is founded, and sedulously inculcating these upon the young entrusted to their charge, are being thoroughly informed of its contents and meanings; for it is already being read in all their Churches. Those, whose principle it damns as detestable and wicked, will come to the knowledge of it more slowly, feeling, even if Free-Masons, little interest in a Papal Bull against Free-Masonry, and little inclined to read so long a paper; and slow to believe that it is an attack upon the civil institutions and system of government under which they live. But they will well understand it by and by, and have something to say in regard to it.

It makes it to be of divine obligation for every faithful Catholic in the United States, to be at heart the mortal and uncompromising enemy of the principles and spirit, the plan and purpose, of the Government under which he lives, and whose equal laws permit him to plot and conspire against it with impunity. It proclaims it to the devout believer as a truth spoken by the mouth of God, that the great axiomatic principles, dear to the lovers of human liberty in every age, dear especially, dear beyond price or expression, to the people of the United States, on which, as upon the immovable adamant of eternal truth, their system of government is builded, are false and criminal and wicked, making the United States to be a part of the Kingdom of Satan.

It makes it his and her duty, therefore, to do all that it may be possible to do to eradicate these principles and destroy all that is builded upon them; to gain control, so far as possible, of the education of youth and convert the young to the Catholic faith; to win or buy for the Catholic Church a power and influence in the government of the country.

Already the Encyclical Letter is acted upon as a political manifesto in Ireland.

Archbishop McCabe, we are told, has written a letter with reference to the approaching election of Lord Mayor for Dublin. He says he is unable to understand how Catholics could in honor and conscience cast their votes for Mr. Winstanley, who is both a Home Ruler and a Free-Mason. "As a Free-Mason he is a member of a society which aims to overthrow religion. To Free-Masonry the revolutions of the last century were traceable. No one can plead non-participation as long as he remains a Mason."

And Mr. Winstanley has repudiated Free-Masonry to obtain votes; and he has been defeated.

But, - for which thanks be unto the God of Hosts "from Whom all glories are"! - Free-Masonry is mightier than the Church of Rome; for it possesses the invincible might of the Spirit of the Age and of the convictions of civilized Humanity; and it will continue to grow in strength and greatness while that Church, in love with and doting upon its old traditions, and incapable of learning anything, will continue to decay. The palsied hand of the Papacy is too feeble to arrest the march of human progress. It cannot bring back the obsolete doctrine that Kings reign by divine right. In vain it will preach new Crusades against Free-Masonry, or Heresy, or Republicanism. It will continue to sigh in vain for the return of the days of Philip II and Mary of England, of Loyola and Alva and Torquemada. If it succeeds in instigating the Kings of Spain and Portugal to engage in the work of extirpating Free-Masonry, these will owe it to the speedy loss of their crowns. The world is no longer in a humor to be saddled and bitted like an ass and ridden by Capuchins and Franciscans. Humanity has inhaled the fresh, keen winds of freedom, and has escaped from companionship with the herds that chew the cud and the inmates of stables and kennels, to the highlands of Liberty, Equality and Brotherhood.

The world is not likely to forget that the infallible Pope Urban VIII, Barberini, set his signature to the sentence which condemned to perpetual imprisonment, to adjuration and to silence, Galileo Gililei, who, it is known, avoided being burned at the stake by denying on bended knees the deductions of positive science, which demonstrated the movement of the earth; and on the 2d of July, 1633, the Cardinal of Santo Onofio Barbering in the name of the Pope his uncle, announced to the world the condemnation of Galileo by an Encyclical Letter, from the Latin whereof we translate these words: "For which matter Galileo, accused and confined in the prisons of the Holy Office, has been condemned to adjure the said opinion...."

Nor are Free-Masons likely to forget that when the Bull of Clement XII, which Leo XIII now revives and re-enacts, was published, Cardinal Firrao explained the nature of the punishments which were required to be inflicted on Masons, and what the kind of service was which the Pope demanded from "the Secular Arm."

"It is forbidden," he says . . . "to affiliate one's self with the Societies of Masons . . . under penalty of death and of confiscation of goods, and to die unabsolved and without hope of salvation." Who will be audacious enough to censure us for replying defiantly to a decree which, by revivor of the Bull of Clement, condemns every Free-Mason in the world to death and confiscation, and damns him in advance to die without hope of salvation?

The world has not forgotten that when Charles IX of France and the Due de Guise at first disowned responsibility for the massacre of 20,000 Protestants, and others, on the Eve and after the Eve of St. Bartholomew, the Catholic Clergy assumed it. Heaven adopted it, they said: "it was not the massacre of the King and the Duke: "it was the Justice of God." Then the slaughter recommenced, of neighbor by neighbor, of women, of children, of children unborn, in order to extinguish families, the wombs of mothers cut open, and the children torn from them, for fear they might survive. "The paper would weep, if we should write upon it all that was done."

Men remember that at Saint-Michel, the Jesuit Auger, sent thither from the College of Paris, announced to Bordeaux that the Archangel Michael had made the great massacre, and deplored the sluggishness of the Governor and Magistrates of Bordeaux. After the 24th of August there were feasts. The Catholic Clergy had theirs, at Paris, on the 28th, and ordered a jubilee, to which the King and Court went, and returned thanks to God. And the King, who proclaimed that he had caused Coligni to be killed, and that he would have poniarded him with his own hand, was flattered to intoxication by the praises and congratulations of Rome. Do men not remember that there were feasts and great gaities at Rome on account of the massacre? That the Pope chanted the *Te Deum Laudamus*, and sent to "his son," Charles IX, (to win for whom the whole credit of the massacre, the Cardinal of Lorraine moved Heaven and Earth), the Rose of Gold, That a medal was coined by Rome to commemorate it; and that a painting of the bloody scene was made, and until lately hung in the Vatican ?

Free-Masonry is strong enough, everywhere, now, to defend itself, and does not dread even the Hierarchy of the Roman Church, with its great revenues, and its Cardinal Princes, claiming to issue the Decrees and Bulletins of God, and to hold the keys with which it locks and unlocks at pleasure the Gates of Paradise. The Powers of Free-Masonry, too, sending their words to one another over the four Continents and the great Islands of the Southern Seas, colonized by Englishmen, speak, but with only the authority of reason, *Urbi et Orbi*, to men of free souls and high courage and quick intelligence.

It does not need that Free-Masonry should take up arms of any sort against the Church of Rome. Science, the wider knowledge of what God is, learned from His works; the irresistible progress of Civilization, the Spirit of the Nineteenth Century; these are the sufficient avengers of the mutilations and murders of the long ages of the horrid Past. These have already avenged Humanity, and Free-Masonry need not add another word- Except these - that there are two questions to be asked, and answer thereunto demanded of all Roman Catholics in the United States, who are loyal to the Constitution of Government under which they live, patriotic citizens of the United States:

Do not your consciences tell you that what is now demanded of you by Pope Leo XIII, by the General of the Jesuits and Chief Inquisitor is, to engage actively in a conspiracy against that Constitution of Government, and the principles on which it is founded; after the dethronement of which principles that Constitution of Government could not live an hour?

If you cannot see it in that light, do not your consciences and common sense tell you, that to approve and favour and give aid and assistance to an open conspiracy against every other Republic and every Constitutional Monarchy in the world, and the principles on which they are founded, is to play a part that is inconsistent with the principles that you profess to be governed by here, is in opposition to all the sympathies of the country in which you live, and is hostile to the influences of its example among the people of other countries, treacherous to your own country, and unworthy of American citizens?

You will have to answer these questions; for they will not cease to be reiterated until you do; and not by Free-Masonry alone.

Given at the Grand Orient aforesaid, the first day of August, 1884, and of the Supreme Council the, 84th year.

The Grand Commander,
ALBERT PIKE, 33d

The Bonseigneur Rituals
Edited by Gerry L. Prinsen
Foreword by Michael R. Poll

8x10 Softcover 2 volumes 574 pages
Retail Price: $54.95
ISBN 1-934935-34-4

This work is a rare collection of 18th century New Orleans Ecossais Masonic Rituals. Included are a photographic reproduction of the original handwritten French ritual, a French transcription and English translation. The work provides a valuable link in the understanding of the development of both Louisiana Masonry as well as the Ancient and Accepted Scottish Rite. This collection is indispensable to any serious study of early Masonic rituals. Two volume set.

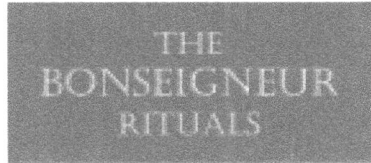

More Light - Masonic Enlightenment Series
Edited by Michael R. Poll
6 x 9 Softcover 194 pages
Retail Price: $16.95
ISBN 1-934935-36-0

This is the a follow-up to the popular book "Masonic Englightenment." Includes the inspired Masonic essays: "Mythology and Masonry" by R.J. Meekren; "Geometry of God" by Joseph Fort Newton; "The Suppression of the Order of the Temple" by Frederick W. Hamilton; "Was William Shakespeare a Freemason?" by Robert I. Clegg; "The Religion of Robert Burns" by Gilbert Patten Brown; "Hysteria in Freemasonry" by WM. F. Kuhn; "The Square and the Cross" by A.S. MacBride; "Toleration and Freethinking" by H.L. Haywood and more.

The Freemasons Key
Edited by Michael R. Poll
6 x 9 Softcover 244 pages
Retail Price: $18.95
ISBN 1-88756-097-1

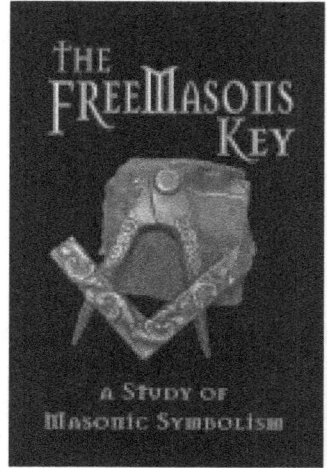

Symbolism is the language of Freemasonry. But what is symbolism? Why does
Masonry use it? Who else has used symbolism? Some of the great minds in Masonic history (Albert Mackey, Joseph Fort
Newton, Oliver Day Street, H. L.
Haywood and more) answer these and
other questions concerning the Masonic
method of teaching as well as explain the symbolism of the Masonic
degrees. This is an indispensable work for anyone seeking to better
understand Freemasonry and its practices.

Review by Edward L. King

"Mike Poll has developed a keen sense of 'what's needed' in the publishing of
Masonic books. In this work, he's filled a HUGE gap that has existed practically
forever.

When one becomes a Mason, the very first thing they want to learn about is
'symbolism'. What does it all mean? What's behind it all? For several decades, the
standard work to address these emergent questions has been Allen Roberts' The
Craft and Its Symbols. This book will not take its place but it should easily become
the SECOND reference for a new or inquiring Masonic mind. While Roberts has
addressed the basics, relating them to each degree in a logical, patterned order, this
work expands FAR beyond that and joins together essays from the best and bright-
est minds from the history of Freemasonry into a book which expands the richness
of our symbolism in detail. Having these all in one easily handled volume makes it
just SO much easier!

This is not to say that these essays themselves are easy: they are, for the most
part, ones to which you will return again and again over the years, each time finding
new gems of thought-provoking stimulation. They approach the subject of Masonic symbolism from varying angles, allowing the rich prism to shine and glow in
your mind.

This is a book that has long been needed: I urge ANY student of Masonic
symbolism to add it to their 'read this now' list and to their library immediately."

Outline of the Rise and Progress of Freemasonry in Louisiana

by James B. Scot
Introduction by Alain Bernheim
Afterword by Michael R. Poll

8x10 Softcover 180 pages
Retail Price: $24.95
ISBN 1-934935-31-X

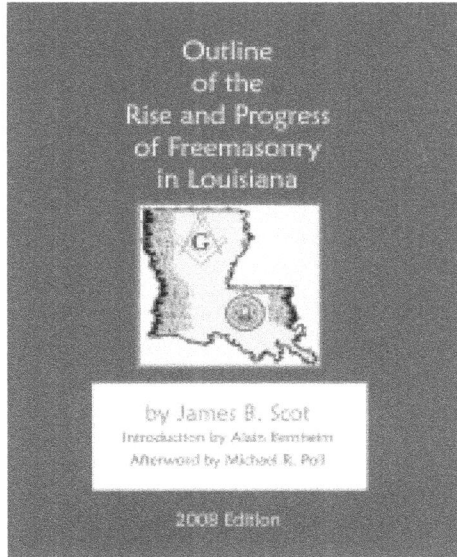

This facsimile reproduction of the 1873 first edition is the granddaddy of modern Louisiana Masonic history books. Scot traces Louisiana Masonry from the organization of Perfect Union and Etoile Polaire Lodges until approximately 1870. Bitingly hostile remarks towards James Foulhouze (some taken from the works of Albert Pike) show the highly emotional climate of Louisiana Masonry in the late 1800's. While Scot sometimes allowed his emotions to get the best of him (slanting his objectivity), this long out of print work gives many valuable bits of information concerning the development of all branches of Louisiana Masonry. The Introduction, by Alain Bernheim, and the Afterword, by Michael R. Poll, are themselves significant Masonic historical works which add greatly to the collected knowledge of early Louisiana Masonry.

The Grand Orient of Louisiana
A Short History and Catechism of a Lost French Rite Masonic Body
Introduction by Michael R. Poll
Softcover 52 pages
Retail Price: $14.95
ISBN 1-934935-23-9

An amazing look into a forgotten Masonic body existing in New Orleans during the late 1800's and early 1900's. The Grand Orient of Louisiana was created to accommodate those working in the French Rite of Freemasonry in Louisiana. This rare work offers important information on the organizational structure and catechism of this unique Louisiana Masonic body. This is in indispensable book for any student of Freemasonry.

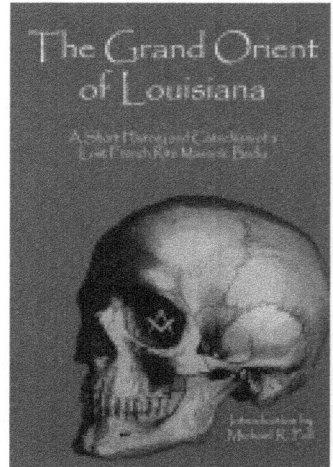

The Schism Between the Scotch & York Rites
by Charles Laffon de Ladébat
6x9 Softcover 66 pages
Retail Price: $14.95
ISBN 1-934935-33-6

In 1850, everything changed for Louisiana Freemasons. Gone was the European style of Freemasonry as practiced by the Grand Lodge of Louisiana since its creation. By force, Louisiana was made to conform to the style of Masonry used by the rest of the U.S. Grand Lodges. This 1853 publication by Charles Laffon de Ladebat shows the emotion, frustration, confusion and pain experienced by the Creole New Orleans Masons as a result of the Masonic "war" that was inflicted upon them.

Lectures of the Ancient and Primitive Rite of Freemasonry
by John Yarker
6x9 Softcover 218 pages
Retail Price: $18.95
ISBN 1-934935-10-7

Lectures
of the
Ancient and Primitive Rite
of Freemasonry

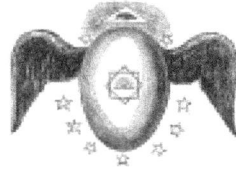

by John Yarker

John Yarker provides a valuable resource for the lectures and catechisms of the Ancient and Primitive Rite of Freemasonry. Lectures of the Chapter, Senate, and Council, according to the forms of the Ancient and Primitive Rite, but embracing all Systems of High Grade Masonry.

Our Stations and Places - Masonic Officer's Handbook
by Henry G. Meacham
Revised by Michael R. Poll
Softcover 164 pages
Retail Price: $16.95
ISBN 1-887560-63-7

Our Stations
And Places

Masonic Officer's Handbook

Revised Edition

by Henry G. Meacham
Revised by Michael R. Poll

One of the most respected Masonic officer's handbooks has been revised for the 21st century Freemason. The various stations of the lodge are examined and practical suggestions are offered to help each officer best perform his duties. This revised and updated edition has been expanded to include a new section for the various lodge committees. This is an indispensable tool for all Lodge officers.

"If it was up to me every lodge should have a collection of these books on hand for every officer to read before the installation so he is well aware of what is expected of him in the upcoming year."
Cory Sigler, *The Working Tools Magazine*

Robert's Rules of Order: Masonic Edition
Revised by Michael R. Poll
Softcover 212 pages
Retail Price: $17.95
ISBN 1-887560-07-6

A Masonic bestseller!

Experienced legislators, editors, civic leaders, business executives, and club officers all pronounce Roberts Rules of Order the best parliamentary Guide in the English language. Its amazing acceptance entitles it to the claim of being the recognized authority in parliamentary law. Now, for the first time, the most comprehensive, understandable, and logical guide to smooth-running meetings has been revised for use in Masonic lodges and appendant bodies.

This is a must for every Masonic lodge officer.

"I strongly recommend this book to all Worshipful Masters, and those who will be in that position, and those who have been but are still interested in helping their Worshipful Masters." -Paul M. Bessel, Past Senior Grand Warden of the Grand Lodge of Washington DC

"I have used W. Bro. Michael's Masonic edition with much success in guiding the affairs of Masonic organizations. I have also used the Masonic edition to mediate disputes. I have even used the Masonic edition in a legal/evidentiary context in court proceedings. While W. Bro. Michael's Masonic edition of Robert's Rules of Order is not binding law in many Masonic jurisdictions, the Masonic edition of the Rules is a helpful guide for the efficient administration and governance of a fraternal organization.

The Masonic edition of the Robert's Rules of Order is an excellent tool for any Masonic organization. I recommend it to every Masonic organization that enjoys peace and harmony in the governance of Masonic affairs."

-Marc Conrad, PM, Asst. Grand Attorney, Grand Lodge of Louisiana, F&AM

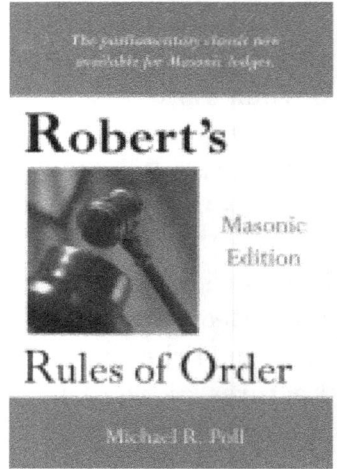

Masonic Words and Phrases
Edited by Michael R. Poll
Softcover 116 pages
Retail Price: $12.95
ISBN 1-887560-11-4

New Masons quickly learn that many unfamiliar words and phrases are employed in our symbolic teachings. Our words are not haphazardly selected, but have deep symbolic and historic significance.

Masonic Word and Phrases is a wonderful collection of the most often used words and phrases in Masonry. Presented in an easy to read and understandable format, this work provides any student of Masonry with a clear understanding of the meaning of our many phrases and words so seldom used outside of Masonry.

This work is valuable to the experienced Mason as a quick and handy reference guide. For the new Mason, however, it is an indispensable work and one that should augment any Masonic education program.

Review

"Many of the words and phrases used in Masonry were borrowed from the craft guilds, from other languages, or from the philosophical vocabularies of the day. This book (which makes a fine companion book to "Masonic Questions and Answers," shown above, provides brief but clear explanations of many of the terms used in Masonic tradition and ritual. Often, Brother Poll goes beyond a surface meaning to show the history of the word, which makes it a richer experience. For an example, consider the entry for "Token." This is from the Greek "deigma," meaning "example" or "proof" - the origin of the word "teach", and in its original sense had much the same meaning as sign or symbol, for it was an object used as a sign of something else. It is generally used, however, in the sense of a pledge or of an object which proves something. In our usage, a token is something that exhibits, or shows, or proves that we are Masons the grip of recognition, for example.

This is one of those basic books that belongs in every Lodge library."
    - Jim Tresner, Book Review Editor, *The Scottish Rite Journal*

Masonic Enlightenment
The Philosophy, History and Wisdom of Freemasonry
Edited by Michael R. Poll
6x9 Softcover 180 pages
Retail Price: $18.95
ISBN 1-887560-75-0

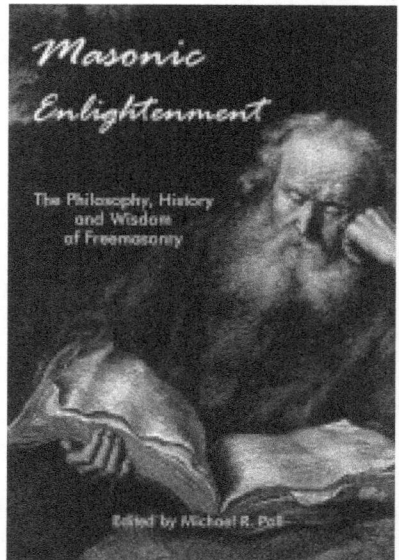

A Masonic Bestseller

A Masonic education from the first page to last. Includes: "The Meaning of Initiation" by Frank C. Higgins; "Operative Masonry: Early Days in the Masonic Era" by Robert I. Clegg; "Masonic Jurisprudence" by Roscoe Pound; "Freemasons in the American Revolution" by Charles S. Lobingier; "A Bird's-Eye View of Masonic History" by H.L. Haywood; "Women and Freemasonry" by Dudley Wright; "In the Interests of the Brethren" by Rudyard Kipling; "The Egyptian Influence on Our Masonic Ceremonial and Ritual" by Thomas Ross; "Anderson's Constitutions of 1723" by Lionel Vibert; "The Rise and Development of Anti-Masonry in America, 1737-1826" by J. Hugo Tatsch; "The Spiritual Significance of Freemasonry" by Silas H. Shepherd; "Rosicrucianism in Freemasonry" by H.V.B. Voorhis; "The New Atlantis and Freemasonry" by A.J.B. Milborne; "Masonry and World Peace" by Joseph Fort Newton and more.

Review

Mike Poll has pulled together a variety of essays from past generations and presented them for the enlightenment of Masons today. These are time-tested thoughts and ideas which older members may have encountered decades ago but which newer members may have never seen. Regardless of your Masonic age, you'll find this small book a delight to read. Whether you devour it on a snowy evening or read a single essay while waiting for car repair to finish, you'll find it a perfect companion and WELL worth the price.
- Edward L. King

The Secret Tradition in Freemasonry
by A. E. Waite
2 volumes 6x9 Softcover 926 pages
Retail Price: $69.95
Website Price: $56.95
ISBN 1-934935-13-1

Many say that this 1911 classic two volume set is the most significant work on the esoteric nature of Freemasonry ever written. Waite provides a detailed account of craft Masonry along with the many allied and high grade bodies along with a study of the symbolism and nature of the various rites.

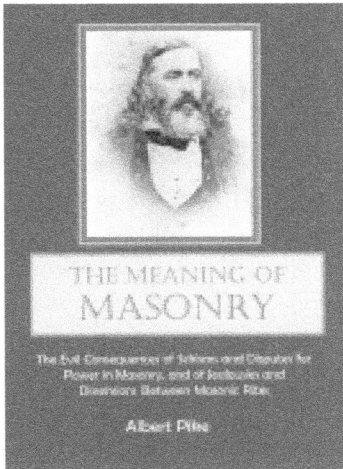

The Meaning of Masonry
by Albert Pike
6x9 Softcover 56 pages
Retail Price: $12.95
ISBN 1-887560-20-3

A biting lecture read at the request of the Grand Lodge of Louisiana, by Albert Pike in 1858. The lecture was subtitled, "The Evil Consequences of Schisms and Disputes for Power in Masonry, and of Jealousies and Dissensions Between Masonic Rites" and is a fascinating look at Pike's interpretation of the "Masonic wars" of the mid 1800's in Louisiana.

Morals and Dogma of the Scottish Rite Craft Degrees
by Albert Pike
Foreword by Michael R. Poll
6x9 Softcover 152 pages
Retail Price: $14.95
ISBN 1-887560-86-6

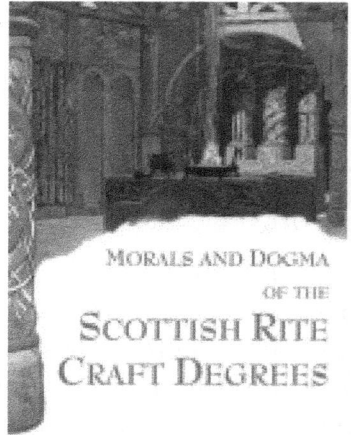

MORALS AND DOGMA
OF THE
SCOTTISH RITE
CRAFT DEGREES

Albert Pike

The philosophy of the Entered Apprentice, Fellowcraft and Master Mason degrees of the Ancient and Accepted Scottish Rite are explored, analyzed and interpreted in this work by Albert Pike. The AASR student will find much food for thought in this craft lodge section from Pike's classic "Morals and Dogma." A valuable and inspired work.

The Lodge of Perfection
by Albert Pike
Foreword by Michael R. Poll
6x9 Softcover 152 pages
Retail Price: $16.95
ISBN 1-934935-13-1

The degrees of the Lodge of Perfection are often viewed as the heart of the Scottish Rite. In these degrees, Albert Pike explores human relations, responsibilities and moral codes. We learn of how humans should interact with each other, how we should govern ourselves and live within our communities. "The Lodge of Perfection" provides each Masonic student with a collection of reflective philosophical lessons which can be used to grow as both a Mason and a member of the human family. The text has been somewhat modernized making an easier reading experience.

www.ingramcontent.com/pod-product-compliance
Lightning Source LLC
Chambersburg PA
CBHW021621270326
41931CB00008B/812